Time 2 Break Free

Tosin Ogunnusi

ISBN: 1-912547-14-7
ISBN-13: 978-1-912547-14-2

DEDICATION

Time 2 Break Free is dedicated to my wife (Anna Ogunnusi) and our children (Leon & Nathan Ogunnusi) for their inspiration, guidance and teachings. It's their unconditional love and light that has allowed me to break free of my own limitations. They continue to challenge me to be a better person every single day. Thank you Anna, Leon and Nathan.

Book Review By Pam Featherstone:

I met Tosin Ogunnusi, the author, several years ago. I was working as a business coach and wanted to have more impact and influence. To do this, I needed to reach out to large audiences rather than solely working 1:1 with clients.

I am committed to guiding business owners to get control of their businesses so that their life is fun. I realised that the importance of being able to deliver inspiring training to audiences would indeed have far greater impact. As part of my quest to reach more people, I attended an Elite Speakers course to improve my speaking skills and Tosin was one of the key mentors. His speaker training was absolutely brilliant, his energy levels were incredible and his passion for life was really infectious. He was and is one of the most fun people I have ever met in my life. He has incredible intuition into what makes people tick and how to get the best out of individuals and teams.

My 3 key values personally are, commitment, consistency and fun and Tosin ticks every single one of those boxes. His commitment to be the best version of himself and serving others and having purpose in his life is delivered with consistency, energy and passion along with a massive dose of fun.

I later had the privilege to spend a week with Tosin, my son, Zander and 10 of my clients. We immersed ourselves completely for a full week of NLP (Neuro Linguistic Programming) with Tosin, learning NLP along with lots of other mindset and empowerment strategies. It remains as one of the best weeks of my life and I know everyone else who attended the course, feels the same way too.

I was thrilled when Tosin told me about his new book, 'Time 2 Break Free' and I was keen to read it. The book truly captures the essence of that week that I spent with my son and friends/clients. It will give everyone who wants to be the best version of themselves, the knowledge, tools and context to achieve this.

'Time 2 Break Free', will answer your question why you are here and will help you to understand your purpose. It will also help you to understand your mindset and how your mind works and guide you so that you can start taking control of your mind, thoughts and your results. When you read the book, you will get a true understanding of why some people succeed and why others fail and why some people achieve great things whilst others struggle with the same things. It will help those who are stuck and want to move forward and it will give you an understanding of NLP (neuro linguistic programming) so that you can understand on a deeper level how the mind works, the experiences we have through our senses and the importance of communication and how we can make this more effective. 'Time 2 Break Free', will help you to establish habits and behaviours that will assist you to overcome fears and challenges and raise your awareness so that you can move forward with opportunities in your life and truly create the life you want and whatever success you want. Tosin expertly addresses what is holding you back and looks at your emotions and the reason why we do things. With this understanding, it will empower and free you to have a new approach and achieve what you want. There is also a great section about the universal laws and why you need them. I remember reading in Tosin's last book about some of these laws, his book was vibrant and fun and just like I'm sure this book will be too, not only will you work through the book and do the exercises and make the lasting changes that you want to see in your life, but it will also be something that you come back too time and time again as it keeps adding value throughout your life. Tosin will help you to be clear about your identity and who you are. Another great value of the book will be in the section that addresses what drives you, because when we get a clearer understanding of our needs and priorities, we can gain traction and momentum and overcome the emotions that hold us back.

So, if your life is completely perfect and you are exactly the person you want to be, having the fun and success you want to have, and everything is working great for you then this isn't the book for you. If you want to understand how your mind works, what gives you the thoughts and feelings that you have, understand better the values that drive you, find out exactly what success looks like to you and what you want and a clear understanding of your purpose as to why you are here, this book 'Time 2 Break Free' will be exactly what you need to get the success you want and understand who you are, and what you need to do.

Tosin will give you the tools, motivation and support to become your best self and improve and develop.

Tosin mentions in his book, the saying 'In life you are either creating or disintegrating' so if you want to create the life you want and you want to make sure you are working in your flow, there is no time like now to get started with the new you. The quality of your education and your thoughts give the quality of the questions you ask yourself and will determine the quality of the decisions and actions you take which therefore give you the quality of your results and your quality of life. Time 2 Break Free is the book that will help you to get that quality of life that you deserve. Tosin writes in a very open and honest style.

Tosin has a great way of communicating, he has oodles of passion for life, which flow throughout the book and will inspire you as well as give you a deep understanding of human nature and how to get the best out of you. This book is a must read for anyone that is serious about their own personal growth and development.

Pam Featherstone

Globally Awarded Coach

CONTENTS

FOREWORD

I am grateful to be invited to write the foreword for this book, which I think is best introduced via the ever-important concept of 'change'.

Change is the one constant in our world that carries us like floating twigs on the fast-flowing river of time. Every second of our lives, we experience change, which we often fail to notice at a conscious level. Some of us recognise change in large measures through major events, while others notice change in every little thing that happens around them. Regardless of how we perceive change, it is a reality in our lives that fosters us through a process of continuous evolution, at a physical, mental and spiritual level. Therefore, change is best viewed as a friend that closes doors and opens new ones perpetually, leading us from experience to experience.

At any given moment in time, each one of us is living an experience. A family is grieving the passing of a loved one whilst simultaneously, there is jubilation over the birth of a child; an arrival of new life. While all this is happening, a couple is celebrating their wedding, looking at life ahead with love, while elsewhere, a family is breaking up amidst deep anguish. Wherever we are, we see action and experience affecting learning, growth and evolution. Change is the fundamental driver behind creation of events and their myriad of outcomes.

Some of us bind ourselves to the experiences of the past,

seeking refuge and comfort in a world that has been. Others live with anxiety and anticipation of the future, wondering what the river of time will bring next. Then there are those that live every ripple in the river of time, from moment to moment. They immerse themselves in the present and flow through their experiences with freedom. In my opinion, the nature of our inclination towards the past, present or future impacts our ability to consciously harness change. As a matter of fact, we can either, embrace, manage or be the change…the choice is ours to make.

This book, in my opinion, offers helpful tools on how best to work with the body, mind and spirit to engage fully with the present, and draw upon the powerful process of change, with confidence and trust in the fact that we are exactly where we need to be every moment, doing exactly what we need to be doing.

I wish you an enriching journey of learning through *Time to Break Free…*

Dr. Amyn Dahya

ACKNOWLEDGEMENTS

To all my mentors (Bob Proctor, Tony Robbins, Topher
Morrison, Andy Harrington, Les Brown, Jim Rohn, Amyn
Dahya, Pam Featherstone, Aran Curry and Avnish Goyal) all
of these amazing beautiful souls have had a real impact in
shaping the person that I have become... Some more than
others and to all of you I want to say
a huge – THANK YOU!!!

I want to acknowledge Sabrina Ben Salmi for introducing me
to Labosshy and Mayooran Senthilmani of DVG Star
Publishing for editing the book and publishing it.
Thank you all.

Finally, my wife Anna, for her creative ideas in getting the
book written, she was also instrumental in editing and
translating the book into Czech. Thank you for your love,
support and companionship.

INTRODUCTION

It was the 12th of June 2016, the last day of a 7 days Elite Speaker Training event, which was held at the Luxury boutique hotel in Kent, Rowhill Grange Hotel and Utopia Spa.

I was one of 5 Mentors assisting the delegates over the 7 days. It was lunchtime and I was sat down with Roslyn Bell, one of the delegates, on one of the beautiful cut grounds. The whole surrounding area was nestled in the Kent countryside and Rowhill Grange Hotel itself is an impressive 19th century manor house that radiated splendour on every level. Everywhere you looked it was just picturesque.

As we proceed to have our lunch, which was typically assorted sandwiches with crisps and salads, Roslyn asked me a question, or should I say a series of questions that got me thinking and inspired at the same time.

She said, "Tosin you were brilliant today, when Andy Harrington (who was the main trainer and my mentor who was conducting the Elite Speaker training that I was assisting on) asked you on the spot, without any warning or preparation, time to stand up and deliver your version of the content he just shared with us. You just got up and delivered it to perfection. You made it look, sound and feel so easy. How did you get so good at speaking? And for someone from a foreign country like Nigeria and the English language being a second language to you, how did you get here? What's your story?"

"Wow," I said, "that's a lot of questions you just asked? It would take me another 7 days to answer it all." She laughed.

"The short answer to your questions is that just like you are doing right now, here over the 7 days learning new skill sets – I guess that's what I've done, and I have implemented and put the stuff I have learnt into practice. And now I find it a lot more comfortable doing it whenever called upon. The funny thing is that, Andy is also known for challenging and stretching the coaches as well, so we don't get too complacent, therefore, I know to always be prepared to be called upon to demonstrate what he's teaching and it's a good practice for us as well. I believe if you are mentoring others then you should be able to demonstrate the skills as well to a very competent level when called upon. Don't you agree?" She said, "Yes, absolutely."

Lunch came and went, and the event ended with all the delegates graduating as Elite Speakers, now ready to get their message out there to the rest of the world.

That evening on my 3-hour drive back from Kent to Norwich, my mind was working on over drive and I began to reflect on Roslyn's questions - How did you get so good at speaking? How did you get here? What is your story? Whilst I was contemplating the questions, I came up with a question of my own to myself: How did I break free from my poor conditioning as a child who grow up in Africa, born in Lagos Nigeria, to a poor family, where my father had 4 wives and 16 children? Where we had two governing rules whilst we were growing up:

1. OBC (Obey Before you Complain), meaning when something went wrong, you were punished before anyone asks any questions and usually 9 out of 10 times you were innocent and not at fault but you got punished anyway and no one bothers to apologise to you afterwards. This was a regular occurrence on a daily basis.
2. SAP now I will forgive you, if you thought SAP stood for (Structural Adjustment Program) as it's commonly known

but you see in my household it was renamed as (Stomach Adjustment Program), you are lucky if you had 2 meals a day, let alone one meal a day.

You see, the question I asked myself prompted me to reflect to the first day I arrived in the United Kingdom on the 20th February 1992, and it was now 12th June 2016. I have been involved in the personal development industry for close to 24 years then and I asked myself another question -What happened to that 19 years old teenager who arrived in the UK with very low self-esteem, confidence and didn't really believe in himself. The teenager who felt inferior to others and could not even lead a silent prayer in front of 5 people, as he would wish the ground would open up and he could just sink into it? What changed for me? Because, I now run my own company Mpowerment, where I inspire others to give more, be more, do more and have more in their lives by awakening them to the God-given Empowerment that exits and resides within them.

My life has totally changed, and I don't even recognise the 19 years old teenager anymore.

It was through these series of questions that the answers of what I had done to change my life started to come through me and I was inspired to write it down and teach it to others.

Over the remaining days of June 2016, I continued to ask questions of myself and I came up with 7 key principles that I had learnt that really assisted me in breaking free from my old conditioning.

They were:

1. **MINDSET** – learning and having the right mind-set to deliver results.
2. **VALUES** – knowing and having a clear understanding of what was driving me.
3. **SUCCESS** – clearly knowing and defining what it is that I really wanted out of life for myself and my family.
4. **EMOTIONS** – allowing myself to open emotionally and express my negative emotions and letting go of the past so that I can grow.
5. **PURPOSE** – focusing solely on my inner gifts and talents and using it for myself and to serve others in a meaningful way.
6. **LAWS** – understanding universal laws and how they govern our planet and learning to work with the law not against it.
7. **IDENTITY** – Who did I need to become to achieve my goals other than my old limiting identity of myself?

I outlined the solutions I came up with to master these 7 key areas and I called it "Time 2 Break Free Life System" because that's exactly what I had done. I had broken free of all my fears, limiting beliefs and limiting decisions in the past.

I got so excited with the information that I immediately wanted to share it and teach it to other people. And over the following subsequent months I put a lot of work into creating a framework and weekend seminar, where delegates could come and get the education that I had learnt and acquired over 24 years of experience in the personal development arena all distilled into 7 key principles where they too could change, shift and transform just like I have done.

It took about 5 months from idea to delivering my first event 'Time 2 Break Free Bootcamp' on 26th – 27th of November 2016 and we had 30 beautiful souls participate in an incredible experience at the beautiful Park Farm Hotel in Hethersett, Norwich.

The delegates got to also participate in doing some empowerment activities such as board breaking with their bare hand, re-bar bending with the soft part of their throat, paired up with another person and bending the re-bar together, arrow breaking with their throat, glass walking barefoot on broken bottles of beer and wine and finally fire-walking on hot embers of coals measuring anything from 500 – 2,500 degrees Fahrenheit, with their barefoot unharmed.

The shares and testimonial of the delegates who attended the bootcamp were incredible. It was one transformation from one person to another. Without exaggeration, it was literally breakthrough after breakthrough after breakthrough and everyone was blown away at the results they got for themselves.

It was after this event that I thought to myself that there are millions of people out there in the world that I could reach with my message and ultimately help change their lives just as I've done, and these delegates have done and experienced too. I knew right then that I had to write this book.

The truth is writing doesn't come natural to me as English is my second language, but I knew I had to overcome my fear of writing and just put my thoughts and ideas on paper so that others can learn from it.

This book "Time 2 Break Free" is a practical book, written in a simple easy to read style for all ages to enjoy. It's a combination of all the learning, experiences and challenges that I've encountered growing up and thriving to succeed in a world that is volatile, constantly changing, mysterious and full of conflict and negativity both internally and externally. This book is all about breaking free from your old negative conditioning and learning to re-new your mind daily in order to strive and create the reality that you want.

"Time 2 Break Free" is a book for those who want to discover their gifts and hidden talents. Individuals who believe they can give more, be more, do more and have more in this world. It's for people who do not believe in a comfort zone and are looking to constantly expand their comfort zone to be constantly growing. This book is also for individuals, who are sick of being sick and tired of going around in a loop, creating the same realities over and over again - and are now looking for a way out to break out of their nightmare and become fully conscious of who they are and what they are here to do.

This book is really an awakening of the soul to remind people of why they are here and perhaps for the first time expose them to see, even if it's a glimpse of what truly lies within them because the first step to changing anything in their lives is "AWARENESS"!

I believe that everything and everyone has a role to play in life. Life is a jigsaw puzzle and everything and everyone has their own little role and purpose just like the little pieces in a 1000 jigsaw puzzle box. The goal in a jigsaw puzzle box of 1000 pieces is to figure out where all the pieces go, how they fit into the whole picture and the overall significant contribution they make to the whole completion of the picture. If you misplace just one piece of the jigsaw puzzle there is no way in which you can complete that puzzle and all of your effort would have been a complete waste until you find that one piece or replace it by buying a new set.

You see, our role and our purpose in life, is not too dis-similar to that of completing a jigsaw puzzle.

The question that a lot of people are asking is: "Who am I? Why am I here? What is my purpose in life? What am I here to do?"

This would sound like a complete cliché but I'm sure you've heard it, or read it somewhere before, that the answer to all those questions lies within you. It really does but the sad thing is most people are looking for it outside themselves. Nothing exists outside of you – everything exists inside of you.

This book is about re-igniting, re-focusing and re-connecting you back to the God-giving empowerment that exists within every human being on the planet. Once you become aware of this greatness within you then the answers to these questions above are revealed to you.

Then you can now find your purpose and your rightful place in society; where you know what to do, how to do it and you do it well, to serve yourself and others. Now, you're a jigsaw puzzle piece who has found it's calling in life and you slot in easily and effortlessly.

What would you learn from reading this book?

- You will learn how to release and let go of negative emotions such as anger, sadness, fear, guilt and hurt just to mention a few.
- You will become aware of the 8 universal laws and how to align with them so that they work for you.
- You will discover what your true purpose is by gaining a deeper understanding of what we are truly here to do.
- You will learn how easy it is to become a co-creator and start manifesting your dreams.
- You will discover how the mystery of life unfolds by awakening your inner soul and become more consciously aware of yourself, others and the planet as a whole.
- Your will gain an innate understanding of how your mind works and how you can create meaning from events that happen outside of you externally. And more importantly what to do to get a favourable outcome from each event, be it negative or positive.

- You will learn and discover what truly drives you in life so you can align your goals and outcomes accordingly.
- You will come to understand that in life you need to become someone who is contributing to life's growth and betterment or else you will be eliminated from life's flow.
- You will find out for yourself what the will is truly designed for and you'll start to use it to your advantage.

This book is certainly not for you if you feel you are already achieving all that you want and you're comfortable in life and have no desire within you to give more, be more, do more and have more in life.

One of the main reasons why I believe most people need this book now is because most people are battling and wrestling with their inner demons, their old negative conditioning, and they don't know how to turn things around and change it.

Secondly, for the advice of the great Martin Luther King, which was sent to me by one of my mentors, Amyn Dahya, who told me to watch the video clip every time I needed some inspiration. I ended up transcribing the video into one of my daily diaries that I keep by my bedside and I read it constantly:

"This is the most important and crucial period of your lives, for what you do now, and what you decide now at this age may well determine, which way your life shall go. And the question is, whether you have a proper, a solid, and a sound blueprint. And I want to suggest, some of the things that should be in your life's blueprint.

Number one in your life's blueprint should be a deep belief in your own dignity, in your own worth and your own somebodiness. Don't allow anybody to make you feel that you are nobody. Always feel that you count, always feel that you have worth, and always feel that your life has ultimate significance.

Secondly, in your life's blueprint, you must have as a basic principle the determination to achiever excellence in your various fields of endeavour. You're going to be deciding as the days and the years unfold what you will do in life, what your life's work will be. Once you discover what it will be set out to do it, and to do it well. Be a bush if you can't be a tree, if you can't be a highway, just be a trail. If you can't be the sun, be a star, for isn't by size that you win or fail, be the best of whatever you are.

Finally, in your life's blueprint, must be a commitment to the eternal principles of beauty, love and justice.

Well life for none of us has been a crystal stair but we must keep moving, we must keep going. If you can't fly, run. If you can't run, walk. If you can't walk, crawl. But by all means keep moving."

I love his advice, and this is the very reason why people need this book now. So, we can keep moving, growing and learning. Life is all about gaining experiences because when it is all said and done, what truly matters is not the amount of breath you take but the moment by moment experiences that takes your breath away and makes you go "WOW"!

The best way to get the most out of this book is by reading it and completing the exercise within it and then re-reading it over and over again. Then start sharing and teaching its contents to others and you will find yourself starting to internalise the information until it becomes second nature to you. Keep referring to the book and its key messages, chapter by chapter. Treat it as a special gift given to you that you love to use daily, that way you will make the most of this book and the contents within it. Remember, implementation of the ideas in this book is where the true power of this book resides. So, take immediate action on the ideas in this book and it will change the course and direction of your life period.

CHAPTER 1
MINDSET
How Does Your Mind Work?

*"Mind is the master power that moulds and
makes, and man is mind, and evermore he takes
the tool of thought, and shaping what he wills…*

*Brings forth a thousand joys, a thousand ills. He
thinks in secret, and it comes to pass.
Environment is but his looking glass."*

James Allen 1903, As a man thinketh so his he

Have you ever heard the phrase "The Sky is the limit?' I'm
sure you have but I beg to differ. The Sky is not the limit,
"The Mind Is!"

The natural questions that should follow would be

"How does the mind work?
What does the mind work with?"

This is what this chapter is going to focus on and reveal to
you for you to start taking control of your mind and therefore
your results.

Observing nature, it compels all living things to keep moving forward and improving. By that I mean it has evolved over time and is continuing to evolve every single day.

There is a saying that: *"In life you are either creating or disintegrating."*

In other words, whatever is not contributing to the flow of life itself will become eliminated. So, are you growing or are you dying? And what determines whether you are growing or dying, whether you are creating or disintegrating, whether your contributing or just consuming and soon to be eliminated?

Before, I answer those questions above, I believe that this is why human beings have been created with an innate ability to always want to increase in their lives – A better house, car, job, increased salary, run their own business, learn a new skill, language or sports etc. Always looking to improve or develop in some way, shape or form.

If this is true, why then do we have some people succeeding and others failing? If everyone is designed to better themselves why are some able to do it and others struggling with it? Now these are great questions and the answer is very simple "It's the way in which they are using their minds". What do I mean?

The minds of human beings use and works with, thought is a living and breathing thing that is alive. Your thoughts are very potent indeed. Thought is thinking. Most people think they are thinking but they are not. They confuse mental activity for thinking. Mental activity is re-thinking the same thoughts over and over again; whilst real thinking is thinking of new thoughts that you haven't thought of before.

The statistics are always changing depending on the source of your findings. As far as I know there are 60K to 80K thoughts per day according to Deepak Chopra but some say, that's just a conservative figure. Let's just assume it's a lot of thoughts per day per person but that's not the issue here. The real challenging fact is that for most people 95% of their thoughts are of yesterday. What do I mean?

Most people are re-thinking similar thoughts of yesterday, today, worrying about what they should have done or didn't do and would have liked to do; dwelling on issues, problems, challenges or the past – This is what I describe as mental activities. Just going through the motions and not really generating any new thinking, any thoughts whatsoever.

This then leads to the conclusion that the way a person uses his mind (Thought/Thinking) must be "The Difference that Makes A Difference," in terms of one's results, would you agree?

If you and I are born, created, with the same stuff, empowered with the same capability and we are all innately designed for increase in our lives then it must naturally follow that the way in which you have learnt to think and use your mind must be the variable difference here. As in the way you've been, conditioned primarily, by your parents.

If that's the case then if one person can get rich, then you can get rich too. If you knew what the other person did and were prepared to do the same things you too would get rich. It's as simple as that.

It must be true that a rich person must therefore be thinking and using their minds in a way to be rich. Similarly, a poor person must be thinking and using their minds in a way to be poor, right?

This revelation for me came from reading the amazing little green book 'The Science of Getting Rich', by Wallace D Wattles. It stated in the book that the first principle in getting rich is understanding and applying this fundamental truth below:

> *"There is a thinking stuff from which all things are made, and which, in its original state, permeates, penetrates, and fills the interspaces of the universe.*
>
> *A thought in this substance produces the thing that is imaged by the thought.*
>
> *A person can form things in his thought, and by impressing his thought upon formless substance, can cause the thing he thinks about to be created."*

I recommend that you get the book and read it if you haven't already done so. It's a great read.

The more you reflect and meditate on this statement above the more you come to see, hear, feel, smell and taste the truth of it.

For instance, if you observe a child, it sees an image of their parents walking or siblings walking and creates an image of itself walking some day and with this constant image of walking one day inscribed in their little minds they begin to sit up, lie down, roll around; then gradually progress to crawling, holding on to things to support them attempting to stand up and falling back down to standing up unaided and falling back down to taking their first steps and falling back down to eventually taking a few steps successfully then falling down and over a few days or weeks of doing this they begin to walk successfully and permanently with ease and very little effort. Children learn in the early days by observation and imitation of their parents, older siblings and peer groups at school.

You as a grown up, now readily think of what meal you are going to have, and you go about producing it. Thought comes first then you create an image of what it is that you are thinking of, wanting or fancying to eat. Then you go out to the super market and purchase the ingredients and go about cooking it and producing the meal that you have imagined in your mind. As simplistic as this may sound to you, it is how you and I think that creates the behaviour and actions that we take or do not take period.

Cooking a meal that you are familiar with or that you are cooking from a recipe book is exactly the same, as they all start with a thought and your creating an image of it in your mind followed by the action steps taken to bring it about.

That is primarily how your mind works. Now we can look at this in more depth through the study of NLP (Neuro Linguistic Programing)

So, let's explore how your mind works. To do this successfully I would like to introduce you to the art and science of NLP.

What is NLP?

Neuro Linguistic Programming is the study of human excellence. It was created by discovering the minds of great achievers of this world in areas such as Sports, Communication, Business, and Therapy. The people who discovered NLP uncovered the key things these individuals were doing that made them stand out from the rest of the masses. They then modelled and duplicated these key areas of excellence to produce similar results.

By learning the basic skills of NLP, you will gain an in-depth knowledge and understanding about how you and others work. This will give you greater awareness over your own life and greater influence in your interactions with others. Let's break down the acronym NLP further:

Neuro: The nervous system, through which our experience is processed via our five senses.

Linguistic: Language and other non-verbal communication systems through which our neural representations are coded, ordered and given meaning.

Programming: The ability to discover and utilize the programs that we run (our communication to ourselves and others) in our neurological systems to achieve our specific and desired outcomes.

A good definition of NLP would be:

NLP is how to use the language of the mind to consistently achieve our specific and desired outcomes.

Why is it important for you to understand how your mind works? There are many geniuses in the world today that cannot teach others what they know.

Have you ever complimented someone on how good they were at doing what they do and they responded by saying, "Thanks, but I haven't got a clue of how I do what I do? It just seems to come naturally to me." Or here's a classic one for sales people, you ask them "that was a great sales call can you tell me how you got the customer to buy", and their response is usually, "You know mate, I was in the zone and can't even remember what I said. You know what, I'll have to record myself in action and see what it is exactly that I'm doing right."

Just imagine for a minute that you were able to establish all the behavioural patterns that you run and more importantly, figure out how you run them. In other words, fully understand the order and sequence in which you do things that create results in your life. Now you've got a recipe book for your life.

Knowing how your mind works is half the battle because with NLP we're able to discover all the patterns you run in your mind and how you run them. As a result, we're able to assist you in changing them.

This is how we're able to assist many people overcome their fears forever by bringing their awareness levels to how it is they are creating their fears, and how they can un-create those fears for themselves. Think about it. If you discover the patterns you run in creating your Phobias and Fears and you know the order and sequence in which you do what you do, then you are in a privileged position to change those patterns and behaviours to run differently. So, NLP is the cutting-edge tool for the 21st century that is used to shift individuals from a state of disempowerment to a state of empowerment.

In other words, you have the ability to think different thoughts from your old ways of thinking and behaving if you knew how your mind works to creating a particular desired outcome.

Language is very important in communication. The words we use help to describe internally how we are feeling about a situation or event.

The art of language and communication is one that we all must master to be very successful in the 21st century! If you agree with this statement, then follow me through the process of how we communicate language and create meaning to events that happen outside of us. I'm not exploring how we communicate with others here, but I'm expressing to you how you and I communicate with ourselves.

Before any human being can begin to communicate internally, something must happen externally to trigger off that communication, i.e. something must happen outside of the boundary we call us for us to begin communicating with ourselves.

Let's call this an external event. There are varying degrees of events, from small events like someone's birthday, making a meal, attending a seminar etc., to big life changing events like the 9/11 incident in the states, the 7/7 bombings in London, winning the jackpot in the tottery draw, having a baby etc.

As the external event occurs, our nervous system can only gather and process the information received from that event through our five senses:

- **See** – Including the sights we see or the way someone looks at us.
- **Hear** – Including sounds, the words we hear and the way that people say those words to us.
- **Touch** – Or external feelings, which include the touch of someone or something, the pressure, and texture.
- **Smell** – One of the strongest senses that we all possess, which includes how something, or someone smells.
- **Taste** - includes all forms of taste e.g. sour or sweet.

When it comes to communication, the first three - sight, hearing and touch, are more prominent than the last two - taste and smell.

As soon as our nervous system receives the information through our five senses we immediately begin to filter the information. Let's talk about the filters for a moment.

You and I have inbuilt into our nervous system three incredible filters - deletion, distortion and generalization. They are innate in our nervous system to ensure that you and I are a success driven machine, and if we do not discover how they work and function then they could work against us. Not understanding this point is like having a brand-new computer without any manual on how to use it! And this is how most of us are running our minds. By the time I finish elaborating these three filters you might ask yourself - "How come they don't teach this in school, colleges and university?" That is exactly the same question I asked myself when I first discovered this information.

Deletion

The first filter is deletion, let's call it delete for short. According to the book Flow: 'The Classic Work on How to Achieve Happiness' by Mihaly Csikszentmihalyi, you and I have over 2 million bits of information bombarding our nervous system every single second. And according to Dr. Joe Dispenza, this figure is over 4 billion bits of information bombarding our nervous system every single second as seen in the controversial movie, "What the Bleep Do We Know!" Well as far as you and I are concerned that's a lot of information bombarding our nervous system every single second. But I'm sure as you are sitting there reading this e-book; you are not aware of 2 million bits or let alone 4 billion bits of information bombarding your nervous system... Or are you? If you are, then you are from another planet and we would have to inform the men in white coats of your existence! Jokes aside, what would happen to you if you were aware of all this information bombarding your nervous system at any one time? Yes, you will go crazy, information overload. You see our conscious mind can only pay attention to 7+/-2 chunks that is about 135 bits of information before our mind reaches its threshold.

There is a part of our brain called the Reticular Activating System or RAS for short which is responsible for deleting 99.1% of all the information that is coming into our nervous system and leaving us with .9% which is what we call our reality. So, the million-dollar question is: What is it that we are deleting and what are we left with?

Well, before I answer that question, let me give you an experience of how we are deleting things all the time. How much attention are you paying to how your shoe feels on your left foot? If you are honest, none whatsoever! Now become acutely aware of how your shoe feels on your left foot - feel any heat, pressure etc. Now, let me ask you a question: Was the experience of your shoe being on your left foot there before I mentioned it…. Yes or No? Yes, it was! You did not just put your shoe on, did you? Assuming of course that you are wearing some sort of footwear whilst reading this e-book.

Just in case you weren't wearing any footwear for the example above, then permit me to give you another experience that would really cement your understanding.

Do you drive a car? I want you to cast your minds back to the very first time you bought your car - brand new or second hand, it doesn't matter. There you were in your car for the very first time, feeling proud of yourself for acquiring your first car and enjoying that new car smell. There you are driving happily away and out of nowhere a car like yours pops into your focus, and another one, and another one, and another one! And in that moment, you question yourself - "Where are all these cars coming from that are similar to the one I just bought?" Did you experience this before? Almost everyone who drives a car will have experienced this scenario. It's a universal experience!

Therefore, it is important for us to know our desired outcome not just for the big things in life but for the small things as well. It is advised that in any given situation, we must know exactly what we want out of it. In other words, tell your mind what you want it to focus on and just like the cars, it will bring it to your awareness. I'm sure you can see how important this first filter is to us but unfortunately there is a downside to this magnificent gift we have. Let me ask you, the reader, a question... What do most people in our society focus on? Do they focus on what they want or what they don't want? You got it exactly, what they don't want!

And this is what they keep experiencing in their world because as the saying goes, you get what you keep focusing on. Where Focus Goes Energy Flows!

Allow yourself the gift of observing your own thoughts on a daily basis, and just pay attention to the things you are focusing on and experiencing. It will give you a clear indication of what you are deleting and what you are getting.

Distortion

The second filter is distortion let's call this distort for short. When information is received through our senses, we simply change that information in some way. This is what is known as distortion and there are literally only two ways in which we can distort information.

We can either make it worse than it is, or we can make it better than it is. Most of us struggle and have challenges with events that happen to us because we change or distort these events and make them worse than they are in our minds.

All successful people simply see the challenge or the problem for what it is, then they see it better than it is in their minds. Therefore, our ability to distort is nothing more than our ability to use our imagination.

When we read a good book or novel and really get totally engrossed in it, do we create sounds, visuals and feelings for the characters in the novel or book we are reading? Then that is distortion.

Just like deletion, we are always distorting the information we hear or read by invoking our imagination. The key here is not to judge these as being good or bad. It really depends on what and how we distort. Distortion could be favourable or unfavourable. By that I mean it could make you unhappy and paranoid depending on how you distort. Here's a classic example, I was at a seminar where the speaker was giving away 150 places on his weekend event, which cost about £295 per person. There were about 400 delegates at this 3-hour seminar. The speaker mentioned this right in the middle of his presentation, offering 150 places for free for the members of this club if they registered after his talk. About 10 minutes after he had made this generous offer, pockets of the crowd were getting up and leaving the room one after the other.

At one point, we had empty seats all over the place and there must have been less than 100 people left. At this stage you could see the strange look on the speaker's face, gazing with amazement and wonder as to why all these people were suddenly leaving the room while he was still talking and well into his presentation.

He quickly jumped to a conclusion, assuming a motive with little evidence and he surprised the rest of the delegates with his interpretation of what he felt was the reason for everyone leaving the room. He felt that he may have said something offensive or that they were leaving because he was boring them. Just then a seated member of the audience said, "They are leaving the room to register for your weekend event." It was at that point that he breathed a sigh of relief and said out loud to himself, "An important lesson for you to learn Jim, next time only make your special free offers at the end of your presentations. Otherwise you will lose more than half of your audience!" Everyone laughed!!!

Generalization

Third filter is generalization let's call it generalize for short. We always generalize; we all do it all the time. Did you pick up any generalizations in those statements? Generalization is when we take a single example to represent a whole group.

This is where our entire ism's come from as in sexism, racism etc. The statement that Black people are a certain way or Asian people are a certain way or Caucasians are a certain way are all gross generalizations. For example, let's say I grew up as a child in Nigeria and my dad treated my mum in a particular way. Now, I take that to represent how a man should treat his woman. So, going from one example to a general conclusion, one would use generalization. It is very useful for learning as it takes what we already know and links it to the unknown. Contemplate this for a minute. Have you ever tried to teach someone something new or tried to learn something new yourself and found you just didn't get it; until the teacher linked it to something you knew or was familiar with and then suddenly you got it in that instant? Or you said to the person you were teaching who didn't get it the first time round, "Ah Bob, this is a bit like playing football", then they say, "Yeah, I get it now, it all makes sense." Our beliefs are generalizations. They give us the opportunity of predicting outcomes in our world based on what we have experienced in the past.

Generalization could be hazardous when:

- We generalize from an experience in a strange way and expect all future instances to fit the same pattern.
- We generalize accurately at the time and create a rule, but neglect to pay attention to the exceptions. The exceptions do not prove the rule – They discount the rule.

People who generalize a lot will be great at seeing patterns and general principles behind specific instances, but they may tend to "Pigeon-Hole" their world and put everything into boxes, fixed categories, and be inflexible in their thinking.

The key here is to be flexible in our thinking approach. A bit like a scientist who creates scientific laws by taking a best guess or an approximation based on his or her present knowledge. We on the other hand do not treat our beliefs in the same manner, as a scientist would do a scientific law. The reason for this is we take our beliefs to be true without questioning why we believe them to be true. And we pay attention to situations and circumstances that confirm them to be true, but we often ignore or dismiss any experience that challenges what we believe. Funny, that isn't it?

To recap, as the event occurs outside of us, we instantly begin to filter that event by deleting, distorting and generalizing the event based on our past experiences, which is based on the psychology - values, beliefs, habits and decisions, we have adopted. The instant we filter the event, we create something in our minds. We create an internal representation, or better said an internal re-presentation of the actual event. This is what we term as our reality of what we think the event means to us.

The meaning we give to events directly affects our emotional state. And our emotional state in turn directly affects our body. The body also affects your state, which in turn affects your mind, your internal representation. This is what is known as the mind body connection or the body mind connection; both mind and body are linked via our emotional state. Allow me to explain in detail with examples to illustrate the point:

Mind Body Connection

I want you to stand up, put your feet together and have both your arms stretched out in front of you in line with your chin and have your palms facing up-wards. Now, (once you have read this!) I want you to close your eyes and begin to use your imagination. Now imagine that on your right hand, someone is placing 30 hardback books, which are of 2000 pages each on your hand one by one, and with each placement the books feel heavier and heavier. Now on your left hand imagine someone tying around your wrist 2000 helium balloons and as the wind blows the balloons up in the air, your left hand begins to lift, lifting, lifting, lifting in the air. Stop now.

Keeping everything just the way they are, open your eyes to see if there is any difference between your right hand and your left hand. Try this now: If there is any difference between your hands, then you have proof of the Mind Body Concept. You see, the mind is the activity and the body are the manifestation of that activity.

What are we really saying? If you are a jealous person and you create pictures or images of your partner cheating on you, then these thoughts, even though they may not be true, will affect your state, which will in turn, affect your physical body or the way in which you will use your physical body. The images, pictures, sounds, tastes, smells and internal dialogues we have and create in our minds are very important. If you create negative thoughts, then you will have a negative feeling, which will in turn predetermine how you will use your physical body to assist you in creating or bringing into reality what it is you are feeling emotionally and vice versa.

Body Mind Connection

Have you ever felt down, maybe because someone just left you; or you have just heard some sad news; or you just couldn't be bothered to do anything; or you just had a row with your mother, spouse, partner, girlfriend, best friend etc.? Then you decided to go to the gym, even though you didn't feel like it, but you dragged yourself along anyway. You start exercising, using the warm up mat to stretch, then the treadmill for running, then the rowing machine to work all those muscles, and then you move on to the dumb bells for a light tone work out. All the while you were listening to your favourite music whilst exercising. Then, you stretch again, use the hot tub, steam room have a great shower and head home feeling much better than you felt before you went to the gym.

So, what really happened there? Moving your whole body differently affected your emotional state, which in turn affected your Mind. The way in which you use your body has a dramatic effect on your emotional state and therefore affects how you think. You see, people don't get depressed, they "do" depression by the way they use their bodies. If you were feeling low and down and you were to play your favourite music and begin to dance, I guarantee you will feel better instantly. Or if you watch your favourite comedy show which gets you laughing to the point of tears, this will instantly alter your state, which will in turn affect your thinking.

As human beings there are only six things you and I can do in our minds and that is: we can hear sounds, we can see things, we can feel feelings, we can taste things, we can smell things and we can talk to ourselves, an internal dialogue. This is how your mind works!

Communication Model

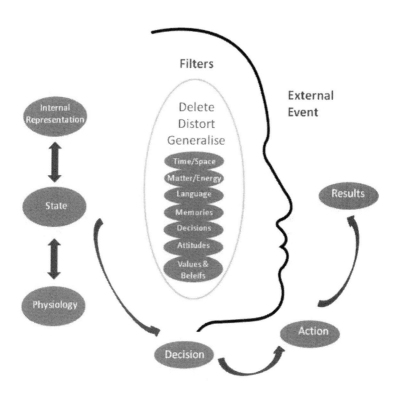

An event happens; we take in the information through our five senses. We then filter the information by deleting, distorting and generalizing the information based on our conditioning, i.e. our values, beliefs, memories, past experiences, etc.

After which, we create an I.R, internal representation, or what is known as an internal re-presentation of the external event. This is the point where we give the event a meaning, what it really means to us. The meaning, good, bad or indifferent will affect our emotional state, which in turn will affect our body. Our body is the medium for expressing our emotions. This is the point where we decide upon what we are going to do because of the meaning we've created and what the decision is going to be. Then, we act with our physical body based on the decision we have made and when we take action, we get a result.

If you are not happy with the result you are getting, then using NLP we can help you to change it. Since the I.R you have created is not real, then NLP can assist you in creating a different I.R. Thereby creating a different meaning to the same event, which will in turn make you feel better and allow you to use your body differently to create a different behaviour, which will in turn get you a different result.

I mean think about it, if you and I cannot truly comprehend or process all the things that are happening around us and we are deleting 99% of what is actually there, and we are only left with 1% of what we call reality, then whatever we perceive must be a lie. So, I ask you, what lie do you want to believe? The one that will disempower you and leave you stuck and rigid in your behaviour or the one that will empower you and give you movement and greater flexibility in your behaviour. Which one? You choose!

This sounds very simple so far and it is, but it is not easily achieved. The one area you and I must make major mental shifts in, is in our old conditioning. You and I will not make any changes to our results if we do not first make the changes in our old conditioning. We need to alter our values, beliefs, decisions, habits, actions etc. There is no doubt that some of these values, beliefs, habits, actions and decisions have been very useful for us while growing up and have truly served us well in the past.

Now, some of these things are the very things that are holding us back, making us very rigid and putting us in a stuck state. The trouble is, a lot of us are not prepared to adopt a different value, belief, habit or make different decisions that will allow us to grow and move forward. There is a saying in business, "The very thing that got you success is not going to keep you there." If you are still running your business the same way you were 6 years ago then eventually you may go out of business if you are not already. We cannot rely on past success, we must keep improving and try to do things differently, more quickly and more efficiently.

There are only two questions we need to ask ourselves and they are:

1. Am I able? It is said that human beings have infinite potentiality, which probably means, no beginning and no end. Therefore, you and I can give, be, do and have anything we want. We can liken ourselves to energy, which is what we are. We can transform from one form of energy to another just as water can be transformed into air.

2. Am I willing? Am I willing to do whatever it takes to achieve my desired outcome, to change that habit, to alter that old belief that's no longer serving me etc.? The minute you say yes, you will be well on your way to creating the life you deserve and eliminating fear from your life forever.

Now, that you've answered these two critical questions, allow me to share with you the 4 Step Solution to acquiring a growth mind-set. It's not enough to understanding how your mind works alone but you must do some internal work and alignment work to ensure you get the best out of your mind. This is what the book is all about – Time 2 Break Free!

Here are the 4 simple steps that I tell our delegates who attend our live weekend 'Time 2 Break Free Bootcamp' through, which is all about adopting a growth mind-set so that you can continue to evolve and experience more of what life has to offer:

THE FIRST STEP - PRIVATE-DIALOGUE

The above process of how your mind works is a detailed explanation of what you do inside your head. This is what I call, Private-Dialogue or something known as self-talk. You have conversations with yourself about what's going on outside of yourself and what it means to you personally and more importantly what you are going to do about it or how you are going to response or react.

There are two distinctive voices in your head one overly critical and the other could be described as overly supportive. The question is which one rules you? Your critical inner-voice or your supportive, inner-voice?

The challenge here is most people do not understand the inner workings of the mind therefore the Succumb to their critical inner-voice and drown out the supportive inner-voice.

The result of this is incongruence, inner turmoil and inner conflict with themselves.

What you need to do is trust, listen and follow through on

what your supportive inner voice is telling you to do. Act on that communication immediately without hesitation and I promise you things will turn out okay for you. Now, don't ask me how – I seriously don't know how but it does.

What is the communication really made up of?

I will tell you, your communication is a composite of your body language, tonality and the words you use. Even though your body language makes up 55% of your communication and 38% and 7% makes up the other two respectively. You can see that 93% of your communication is non-verbal, so even when you are saying nothing at all you are saying a lot.

The key here is to make sure that your body language, tonality and words that you use are all in sync and that is what is known as speaking your authentic truth. The question is how often do you speak your authentic truth?

I challenge you to pay attention to your daily thoughts and how you evaluate them and whether you react or respond appropriately or inappropriately. Adopting some of the strategies and tactics here would go a long way in giving what we call, Emotional Intelligence, which is just a fancy word for managing and taking responsibility for your emotional state.

Let's start you off adjusting some of your old conditioning by introducing you to some new beliefs. As you contemplate these beliefs, you too will begin to think and feel differently about yourself and others. Adopting these as your own will also assist you in building up confidence in yourself and will also assist in eliminating your own doubts, fears and anxieties.

Here they are:

1. Everyone has a unique model of the world: everyone has their own individual beliefs and ideas about how the world works, and about their (and everyone else's) role and relationship in it.

2. Respect everyone's model of the world: you may not agree with someone else's beliefs, values, and way of judging the world and the people in it but respect it. Acknowledge that they have a model and that it works for them (maybe not in an ecological way, and maybe it's partially self-destructive for that person, but it's theirs).

3. The map is not the territory: we have a 'map or a representation of the world and how it works. But it's based on gross deletions, distortions, and generalizations, and bears little resemblance to actual reality. The representation is NOT reality; it is a representation only, and not an accurate one at all. It's like the menu at a restaurant is not the food – it's only a brief and limited description of the food.

4. People are not their behaviours: people are one thing (a collection of values, beliefs, distorted memories, internal representations, lessons, etc.), but their behaviours are how they act. Those behaviours come from all those values, beliefs, internal representations, etc. The behaviour does not define the person, ultimately, but is a moment-by-moment reflection of what the person is at that moment. As a professionally trained NLP Trainer I accept my clients, but work to change their behaviours.

Sometimes that involves changing internal representations, beliefs, etc. in the client.

5. The meaning of all behaviour is dependent upon the context it exists in: a behaviour in one context is negative, but in another context is positive. Someone who yells and acts up in church is seen as being inconsiderate and a lot, but the same behaviour is just having a great time at a rock concert get the idea?

6. All behaviour has a positive intention: at its highest level, all behaviour ultimately aims to preserve and safeguard the life and wellbeing of the person exhibiting the behaviour (and possibly others whom the person values). Even the most destructive acts ultimately are committed because at an unconscious level, the committing of that act is trying to bring about a positive result for the individual.

7. The most important information about a person is that person's behaviour: it's the only thing we can see outwardly, and the only thing the person committing can't lie about, pretend, or cover up. Often, they may not be aware of their own real reasons for the action, or even be aware that they're committing the actions. The behaviour is the only piece of "hard evidence" we have about them. It's like catching someone red-handed whilst they are stealing something in the moment. It's undeniable!

8. Everyone is doing the best they can with the resources they have available: those resources can be internal states, like motivation, happiness, anxiety,

depression, or physical things like money, tools, and other people. We're all trying to do the best we can, given our states, beliefs, internal representations, etc. People with more positive internal representations, beliefs, and tools at their disposal tend to do better than those who are missing even a few key beliefs or internal representations or have destructive ones that are sabotaging what they want to do in life.

9. There are no unresourceful people, only unresourceful states: everyone has the tools that they need to succeed, and if they don't, then they certainly can go out and get those tools. Tools meaning anything from positive internal representations to cash to contacts for getting a movie made. We all started off at zero, as infants. If a person is not out there on the path to accomplish what he/she wants, it's probably because his/her internal representations / beliefs are unresourceful or unhelpful and is hampering them from achieving what it is they want to achieve.

10. There is no failure, only feedback. Failure is really a subjective term. If you perform an action with the intention that you simply want to get better and better at it, then individual acts aren't failures - they're just feedback on your approach and way of doing things and are ultimately stepping stones on the path to getting the results you want.

These are all convenient beliefs and there is no way of proofing whether there are true or false. The only thing I can tell you is that if you take them to be true for you personally, it will improve your results.

Here's another easy and practical strategy you can use to assisting you in shifting, changing or reserving your thought/thinking process.

It's called "Stop, challenge and choose."

Let me explain, whenever you find yourself, entertaining a negative thought in your mind. Tell yourself to stop and recognize the pattern in your thoughts or thinking process.

After that you then challenge yourself and this is called interrupting the pattern; ask yourself, where am I going with these thoughts? How does thinking this way make me feel right now? How emotionally attached or detached am I right now because of thinking this way?

And finally, you choose how you want to feel, react or respond to the thought process. This is about taking full responsibility and choosing a different response. Ask yourself, how do you want to feel in the next 5 minutes instead of how you're feeling right now because of this thought process?

This new pattern of behaviour would allow you to start taking charge of your mind and be in control of the way you think rather than reacting to other people's thoughts and ways of thinking that you have been conditioned to in the past.

Here are some common examples where the "Stop, challenge and choose" technique would be very useful:

Example 1: Your daughter or son has just taken their driving test and you have not heard from him/her long after the test was over; which is very unusual. This is not their typical behaviour.

Example 2: Let's say your mum and dad have just called you and left you a message saying; call us back as soon as possible please.

Example 3: Your partner, spouse, girlfriend or boyfriend was due back from work, about an hour ago and you have not heard from them as yet and this is also very unusual pattern of behaviour.

In all these examples I want you to ask yourself the following questions:

1. What would be your initial reaction?
2. Where did that thought come from?
3. What made you think that?
4. How did the thought make you feel?

Now, think of a time where you created your own meaning to something that was either said to you or that you had seen or you felt.

1. What was your initial reaction?
2. Where did that thought come from?
3. What made you think that?
4. How did the thought make you feel?

Now I want you to apply the "Stop, challenge and choose" strategy to whatever you came up with above.

1. **Stop** – What was the pattern in your thought or thinking process?

2. **Challenge** – What if the negative thought was untrue? What positive thought could you adopt instead? And…
3. **Choose** – A different response. How would that make you feel?

The whole idea here is to assist you in shifting, changing your way of thinking in the moment so you can be more in control of your thought process and choose how you wish to respond and not react to situations and circumstance no matter how they appear to you.

Remember that the quality of the conversations you're having in your head will ultimately determine the quality of your life.

SECOND STEP - ASSUMPTIONS

What are assumptions? Assumptions are simply beliefs that you hold to be true.

So, what's a belief? A belief is a feeling of absolute certainty about yourself, others and the world around you.

The primary key to your success is a bulletproof belief in your self-worth and your own abilities.

I believe it was Henry Ford, who said,

"Whether you think you can or you can't, you are right."

The irony is you and I live in a world of uncertainty and yet we must act as if we have certainty in order to get what we want. It reminds me of a story that one of my mentors shared with me whist attending one of his, "Legacy Trainers Training Program."

I want to share it with you because it sums up this section beautifully:

The Pygmalion Effect

Have you ever met someone who seems to have luck wherever they go? I have a friend appropriately nicknamed, "Lucky." It seems that no matter what Lucky does, or no matter where he goes, good fortune follows him. I'm not just talking about finding pennies on the street. Lucky is the kind of person who can create millions of dollars with ideas that are surprisingly simple yet no one else seems to think of them. It seems that Lucky just happens to meet the right people at the right place at the right time. I remember sitting down with Lucky one afternoon just after I had met him, and I asked him how he got his nickname. His response was as simple as his moneymaking ideas. His answer? "Because I am!"

Why do some people like Lucky seem to have all the luck in the world, while others seem to hit walls everywhere they turn? Have you ever experienced this in your life? What determines why you are on a roll or in a rut? The answer is as surprisingly simple as Lucky was. The answer to this question comes from within you. You are the one that determines whether you are in a rut or on a roll. The important thing for you to find out is how you can more consistently produce the rolls over the ruts. This determinant comes from a dynamic called the Pygmalion Effect, and it's a primary force by which I govern my life. The origin of the Pygmalion Effect is as interesting as the effect itself, it came from Greek mythology.

The story begins on the island of Cyprus. Long ago, in the

city of Amathus, lived the great King Pygmalion. King Pygmalion was an incredible leader and renowned sculptor, but unfortunately a very lonely man. His standards for a perfect mate were so high that he was never able to find a woman who could fulfill all his wishes. King Pygmalion saw so much to blame in women that he resolved to live a solitary life, yet his constant yearning for companionship and love created a great void in his life. No matter where he searched, he could not find true love.

Never able to find this love, one day the King set out to create a sculpture of the perfect woman, and he began with a perfect piece of Ivory. All sorrow and loneliness left his heart as he worked on the sculpture. When he finished, he had created a work of art with such beauty and perfection that he fell in love with it. She was the perfect semblance of every trait and characteristic he had hoped for in a partner, less one - she was of ivory and not of flesh. While indeed made of ivory, his creation was so perfect it looked like the craftsmanship of nature. So real was she, he would place his hands upon her face as if to assure himself that she was still made of ivory, yet even his caress could not convince him it was not flesh. He would bring her daily gifts of love - bright shells, beads, amber, polished stones, forest animals and flowers of numerous hues. He adorned her with amazing treasures - rings for her fingers, earrings, and rare pearls for her neck. He made sure that she rested on the finest of pillows and was warmed with the best of downs.

His passion and love for her was so strong he prayed to the Greek Goddess of Love, Aphrodite to bring her to life. "Ye Gods, who can do all things, give me, I pray you, for my wife, one like my ivory virgin." Knowing that his prayers would be answered, he announced to his Kingdom that he was to wed his creation. Everyone thought he was crazy, and perhaps he was, but he never faltered, and always began and ended his days with prayers to Aphrodite. As the wedding date grew nearer, his advisors urged him to call off the wedding for fear that the King would be made a mockery. Yet his certainty never waned. Instead, he sent his bride to be fitted for a dress and commissioned the finest seamstress to create the perfect gown. Still, everyone talked of his mental instability, and his staff began to grow unfaithful. King Pygmalion began to banish his naysayers and demanded that his entire staff be loyal to the soon-to-be queen as well as to him.

As each day drew nearer to the wedding, everyone watched the King lose his reputation and his power, but never did he lose his faith. Aphrodite was so touched by his intention and certainty, that she raised a fiery point into the air and brought life to his creation. As Pygmalion returned home, he gave his usual kiss to his statue. But this time it felt warm! He pressed the statue's lips once more and laid his hands upon her back. The ivory felt so real, so warm and soft he knew his prayer had been answered; she was indeed alive! The virgin felt his kisses and blushed amid opening her timorous eyes as she fixed her gaze on her lover. Aphrodite then blessed the nuptials she had created, and from their union was born Paphos - a daughter with such beauty a city was named in her honour. To this day, the city of Paphos is recognized as one of the most beautiful cities in all of Greece.

Since then, when someone expects something with so much certainty, and so much conviction that it actually happens, it is called the Pygmalion Effect. This Greek myth describes the power of intention and certainty. Dr. Robert Rosenthal, a researcher from Harvard University coined the phrase, "Pygmalion Effect" after numerous scientific studies concluded the existence of these phenomena, but the inspiration of his studies came from Robert K. Merton, the sociologist who coined the phrase "self-fulfilling prophecy" in a seminal essay published in the Antioch Review in 1948. According to Merton, a self-fulfilling prophecy is an expectation or prediction that is initially false, (remember that later) which initiates a series of events that cause the original expectation or prediction to come true. Merton described this phenomenon as having 3 phases:

1. You have a belief in something (false at the time it is held).
2. You behave in a way you would not have normally done in the absence of that (false) belief in your mind.
3. The behaviours displayed in phase two actually create events, which make the belief then become true.

This dynamic can also work in reverse. It is my feelings that most, not all, of the negative events in the world are created from a "Negative Pygmalion" effect. So many people these days expect to be robbed or mugged, that it becomes a self-fulfilling prophecy. It's not limited to crime either. One of the most powerful examples that Merton argued for self-fulfilling prophecies, now referred to as the Pygmalion effect, was the collapse of a solid and solvent financial institution - the Last National Bank. The collapse began in the early 1930's when a rumour (false at that time) that the institution was on the verge of bankruptcy (phase I). That led to a massive withdrawal of savings by panicked depositors (phase II), which in turn led to the actual collapse of the bank (phase III).

So, back to my friend Lucky. The reason he is, in fact, lucky is because he believes that he is. I realize this may seem too easy on the surface, but the system has been in place since 1948, thanks to Merton. If you want something to happen, believe that it will! Then, behave as if your belief is true, and it may just manifest. Remember - King Pygmalion believed that his statue would come to life, but that wasn't true either.

Have you ever experienced the Pygmalion Effect in your life? If so, I certainly hope it was for the good. If you are experiencing events or situations in your life that you don't want to have happen, ask yourself this: Do you expect them to happen? What are your beliefs regarding the events happening in your life? Remember those people who seem to have nothing but good happen to them? They believe things, too. Ask them if they expect good things to happen, and almost invariably they will say yes. I realize it's illogical, but it works. They seem to be "invincible" to negative happenings and it all begins with a feeling of certainty - a belief.

Now, I realize that this leaves open a huge philosophical debate, and you might well find as many examples in life about how a positive intention "didn't work" for yourself or someone you know. But the truth is, negative expectancy just doesn't serve you or the world. Einstein once said, "I'd rather be an optimist and a fool than a pessimist and right." I guess that's my philosophy too, and one might say I'm crazy for believing in something so strange, but then again, so was King Pygmalion.

I love this story, I hope you did too but here's the key, what you need to explore here is what do you believe in and is your belief serving you by moving you in the right direction or is it holding you back from expressing and being your true self?

Adopt a positive approach to life and create good assumptions in all areas of your life. This will be of great benefit to your overall life and wellbeing.

THE THIRD STEP - NATURE

Would you agree that no man or woman is an island all by himself or herself, yes or no?

The reason for this is that no man, woman or company can be successful all by themselves. They all need other people in support of their goals, desires and dreams in order to fulfill it. Now don't get me wrong, the aspiration and inspiration have to start with you first, 100%, but along that journey in order for you to become truly successful you're going to need other people's support.

If you observe nature very closely you will see how it interacts brilliantly with all the elements within it including us. It's a real phenomenon. Hence why, I had to include this information in my book. It is very essential that we take our time to really understand ourselves and as a result you will notice that people around you are essentially the same. Now they might be getting a different result to you, but the fundamental makes up of who they are at their core is essentially the same.

There are 5 elements in nature and all these 5 elements are within you as well. Hence the saying, all you need is within you. From a simple atom to the cosmic universe – Your whole entire body is just a mini cosmos of the universe itself. Let's explore the 5 elements in nature before I go all, esoteric on you and confuse the hell out of you. My goal here is just to give you a basic understanding of what these elements are and our relationship with them. Here they are:

1. **WATER**

   Water is the first element in nature and 72% of our planet is made up of water according to a mystic from India Sadhguru of the Isha Foundation. Your physical body is also 72% water. Hence why all the nutrition experts say, drink lots of water because just like a river you have to keep the water in your body flowing otherwise it becomes stagnate like a dam. This can cause all sort of issues in your physical body and water is essential for the distribution of nutrients to your body, for blood circulation and for your digestive systems to function properly.

2. **EARTH**

   Earth is the second element in nature and 12% of our planet is made up of earth from the same source above. Our own physical body is 12% earth. Your skin is the limitation of your body or boundaries of your physical body – And all it is, is pure dust, Earth. It is the core element of your physicality and it is one of our greatest limitations if you do not educate yourself as to how it functions. It has become very complex for most people in their lives because they identify with it but how could you not? It's the body you reside in.

3. **AIR**

   Air is the third element in nature and just 6% of our planet is air. Your physical body also has 6% of air in it. This is a very easy one to grasp as you can all breath – By taking a breath in and a breath out. So, everyone can easily take charge of this one element. It is a very essential element of our lives and you can sometimes take it for granted. If there was an unusual phenomenal that could suck out the air in the atmosphere this very minute, everyone and every living thing on the planet would drop dead instantly. This is how vital the air you and I breath in and out is to all living things on the planet.

4. **FIRE**

   Fire is the fourth element in nature and only 4% of our planet is fire. Natural fires in nature could be lightening, volcanoes and bush fires in Australia due to dry weather – Other than man made fires like bombs and missiles. Your physical body also has 4% of fire within it. This is not an element we need to take charge of unless you want to defend yourself from an attack or intentionally burn someone that you perhaps have perceived as harmful to you in some way. And finally ...

5. **SPACE**

   Space is the fifth element in nature and there is 6% of our planet, which is just pure space, not space as in empty space. In the science of getting rich book, this space that I'm talking about is referred to as, "A thinking stuff, from which all things are made, and which, in its original state, permeates, penetrates, and fills the interspaces of the universe." You as a physical being also have 6% of space within you. There is no need for you to explore this space unless you are interested in understanding the mystical aspects of life itself.

The first four elements - water, earth, air and fire, are the main ones we should observe closely and fully understand to really strive in society.

When you observe nature, you can clearly see how it interacts with these four elements in complete harmony and synergy. Just as nature, human begins to interact with each other in a similar fashion because you have all four elements within your makeup.

Every human begin has a unique blend of water, earth, air and fire tendencies or preferences. Your preferences will change from time to time depending on the role you play for example, a parent, a teacher, a manager, a team member, a student, a coach, a customer, a buyer or a seller etc.

Nature or human nature is just a guide for you to interact with others more efficiently and effectively. It's a representation of the whole not the whole itself.

There are so many psychometric analysis nowadays that would make your head spin. Some of the major ones are the NLP Representational System, The 4-Mat Formula or the DISC Model and so on and so forth.

What I like about relating nature and human beings is its simplicity and ease of understanding in comparison to Myers Briggs for example. Yet it is very powerful indeed. Easy to understand, digest and implement for individuals and teams.

It's applicable for your personal and professional lives as well.

The key thing to understand here is that under stressful conditions you have a primary preference for 1 or 2 of these elements to be more dominate in you. So, the real question is what is your human nature?

To answer that question let me highlight the characteristics of each individual elements for you:

WATER ELEMENTS

They value relationships and are very friendly and loyal by nature. They enjoy building rapport with people. They respond well to warm conversation, quite open with others and enjoy building connections. Water elements are usually very quiet and calm individuals. They are people eccentric and like to get along with everyone and would avoid any argument or conflict of any kind. There are relatively quiet and softly spoken.

KEY WORDS:

Empathy, Considerate, Feelings, Relationships, Consideration, Honesty, Friendliness, Support, Sharing, Caring, Calm, Consistent, Trust-worthy, Loyalty, Listening, Service, Serving, Respect, Concerns, Relaxed, Gentle, Helpful, Slowly and Softly, Sympathy, Compassion.

EARTH ELEMENTS

These individuals are very confident in their abilities and

approach. They want the job done quick and properly. They are quick thinking, witty, driven and ambitious. They pride themselves on finding solutions quickly and effectively. They expect a lot of themselves and others and could be very demanding of others. They could be perceived as blunt, aggressive and don't have time for chitty-chatting at all. The earth element individuals are risk-takers they know what they want and why they want it. And in this regard would like to lead the conversation. They are very grounded and solid individuals just like the earth itself.

KEY WORDS:

Decisive, Facts, Solutions, Results, Confident, Direct, Offers, Deals, Bargains, Control, Lead, Firm, Solid, Bold, Blunt, Straightforward, Assertive, Driven, Risk- takers, Quick, Fast, Controlled, Purpose, Delegating, Delegation, Responsibility, Goals, Targets, Outcomes, Significance, Accomplishment, Superior, Knowledgeable, Unique, Special.

AIR ELEMENTS

They are organised and thrive on details and processes that allows them to streamline their work. They like to check and re-check information and value factual or evidence-based approaches. Leave it to these individuals to read all the service manuals and they also ask a lot of questions. There are known for their expert knowledge, thorough demonstration of evidence to back it up. They are meticulous, orderly and focused individuals. They enjoy making lists and proving things.

KEY WORDS:

Counts, Logic, Orderly, Knowledgeable, Knowledgeable, Quality, Information, Proof, Structure, Clearly, sequentially, Accuracy, Needs, Meticulous, Critical, Clear, Thorough, Systems, Procedures, Sharing, Credibility, Questions, Certainty, Routine, Planning, Control.

FIRE ELEMENT

These element individuals are exciting to be around because they are a lot fun. There are the life and soul of the party. They are remarkably optimistic and energetic people who strive on problem solving and seeing the positive impact they have on others. They like the big picture and get excited about new possibilities. They enjoy the company of others but can get bored easily with too much detail in a conversation. They respond well when people resonates with their energy and enthusiasm. These are passionate and energetic individuals. Just like the sun that shines brightly in the summer time - These individuals are very bright that they radiate colour and style. These individuals are easily distracted.

KEY WORDS

Fun, Ideas, Chaotic, Confusion, Spends, Bright, Possibilities, Spontaneous, Enthusiastic, Distraction, Spend, Potential, Excitement, Enthusiasm, Smile, Gadgets, Colour, Impressive, Style, Energy, Speed, Uncertainty, Variety, Drama, Positive, Optimistic, Team, Player, Encouragement, Interest, Hope, Future, Uniqueness, Animated, Emphasis, Popularity,

Recognition.

The goal here is to establish what primary element you are and to figure out how to adapt your behaviour, so you can interact better with all the other elements just like nature does. This is not just essential in your personal lives but it's equally beneficial if not more crucial when working with your teams.

So, what is a company and what is the culture within that company?

For me both answers to the above question are the people within that company as they represent the company, its culture and its brand.

I'm sure you will agree with me that understanding and adapting your natural nature; is essential and a vital necessity in creating the right culture within your businesses.

So, in conclusion here, I would like to leave you with a few questions to contemplate on:

- What is your human nature?

- What are your strengths and weaknesses for your preference?
- How would you approach you?
- How would you not approach you?
- How would you add value to your relationships both personally and professionally?

Now answer these same questions for the other 3 elements and how would you adopt or flex your behaviour to suit the other 3 preferences?

Remember all four elements resides and exists within you and to obtain flexibility, influence and impact on others, you will need to become very competent at tapping into all four elements depending on the individual you are communicating with.

STEP FOUR - EMPOWERMENT

The final piece of the puzzle for acquiring an evolving mind-set is to continually strive to expand your comfort zone by daring yourself to do something you've never done before, or every thought was possible for you – I call this act, "EMPOWERMENT!"

I believe every single one of us has been endowed with the gift of empowerment. So, what is empowerment really? Empowerment is the green light, the go ahead, the permission or license to grow and expand yourself in some unique and profound way.

Too often most people are waiting for other people to validate them before they can do what they need and ought to do in the first place. Perhaps you are one of those people needing validation before you can act.

The truth is you have already been empowered by birth – So, just give yourself permission to do the things you want to do and get on with it.

So, how do you empower yourself?

There are several ways in which you can empower yourself:

1. Do something you've never done before...
2. Take a on a new challenge every year...
3. Embark on a new project...
4. Learn a new language, sport or craft...
5. Travel to a new destination and meet met new cultures yearly...
6. Adopt the C.A.N.I. mantra (Constant and Never-ending Improvement) of yourself.

Any of these activities above will allow you to become aware of valuable resources within yourself that you never thought you had.

When you enrol and attend our 2-day Time 2 Break Free Bootcamp, we empower you by taking you through our empowerment activities known as "BRAG & F", that is breaking wooden boards with your bare hands un-harmed, Re-Bar Bending with the soft part of your throat with a partner or buddy, Arrow Breaking with the soft part of your throat, Glass-walking with your bare foot and finally Fire-walking with your bare foot, walking over hot embers of coals measuring 500 – 1,500 Degrees Fahrenheit.

This empowerment activity together over a weekend has never been done before. The only time you can do all five in one go is if you are learning to become an instructor but at Time 2 Break Free Bootcamp you will be attempting all five empowerment activities, which means you will be experiencing breakthrough after breakthrough after breakthrough as you completely overcome your fears, Although it has been said that you cannot really overcome that which does not exist, and tap into your unstoppable powers that resides within you.

So, this was Private-Dialogue, Assumptions, Nature and Empowerment. The tools, tactics and strategies to discovering and understanding how your mind works – In order to manage your emotional state and develop a growth mind-set.

SUMMARY: MINDSET – HOW DOES YOUR MIND WORK?

- The sky is not the limit, your mind is!
- Your mind works with thought energy, which is alive and very potent indeed.
- Most individuals engage in mental activity and call it thinking. Mental activity is not thinking, it's re-thinking, re-acting based on old conditioning or patterns of behaviour. No new thought is generated from this kind of thinking process.

- Real thinking requires effort and it's one of the hardest things to do, especially when the appearance of things in your life dictates otherwise e.g. being diagnosed with cancer and having to think of being in a healthy state of mind. Being poor and must think abundance and create thoughts to get you out of your situation. That is real thinking.
- You can become RICH by thinking in a certain way and acting in a certain way.
- Disharmony, lack and limitation, discord, poverty is all the result of adopting a negative mind-set, way of thinking and acting.
- Wealth, health, harmonious and desirable conditions and circumstances are obtained by adopting the right mind-set (way of thinking and acting).
- The truth is the world you live in is just a reflection of the world you live inside your mind – As the saying goes, "all you need is within you and given to you from birth."
- Exploring and understand how your mind works is extremely important. Her are the four stages as a reminder:
- Stage 1 - Information comes in through your 5 senses. (Sight, hearing, taste, touch and sense of smell).
- Stage 2 – You process the information in your mind, you have the option to choose, accept or reject that information at a conscious level.
- Stage 3 – Once you've accepted or rejected the thought, you create a meaning for it at the subconscious level. Whatever meaning you've given to the event will affect your emotional or physical state.
- Stage 4 – Your emotions are just vibrations in your body and there are expressed through your physical

body. In other words how you act or behave. This action or behaviour will determine the results you produce, be it good, bad or indifferent.

- If you change the way you think you change the way you feel.
- I want you to adopt the Stop, Challenge and Choose strategy:

1. Stop - What was the pattern in your thought or thinking process?

2. Challenge - What if the negative thought was untrue? What positive thought could you adopt instead? And

3. Choose - A different response. How would that make you feel?

- Assumptions are beliefs you hold to be true. So, what do you believe about yourself, others and the world at large?
- What is the Pygmalion Effect? It is when someone expects something to happen with so much certainty and conviction that it happens.
- What is your human nature? Water, earth, air or fire? Remember you possess all these elements within you. So, be sure to learn how to adopt your nature so that you can get along with others too.
- What is Empowerment? Empowerment is the green light, the go ahead, the permission or license to grow and expand yourself in some unique and profound way. It's doing something you've never gone before and never thought possible for you.

"Your past does not equal your future unless you live there"

Tony Robbins

CHAPTER 2
VALUES – WHAT DRIVES YOU?

*"Without Values there is confusion and chaos.
When Values disintegrates, everything disintegrates.
Health disintegrates. Poverty attains dominance
over affluence, societies and civilisations crumble.
When we pay attention to these values that society
has always held sacred, then order emerges out of
chaos, and the field of pure potentiality inside us
becomes all-powerful, creating anything it desires."*

Deepak Chopra

*"Personal leadership is the process of keeping your
vision and values before you and aligning your life to
be congruent with them"*

Stephen Covey

*"Values are like fingerprints no bodies are the
same, but you leave them all over everything you do"*

Elvis Presley

What are values? Your values are your drivers in life. It's your mental map of how you view yourself, people and the world at large. It's what is really important to you. Values predict your behaviours.

To find out someone's value, watch and listen to them, pay attention to what excites them and what changes their state to one of interest and curiosity. What do they pay attention to? The same goes for you, just observer yourself and you can clearly see what it is that you really value.

If you want to change your behaviour, then you have to change your values. It's just that simple.

Why is knowing your values important? It's vital because everything we do is the result of what we value. If we can identify the order of values as they related to certain areas of our lives like spirituality, career and finance, personal development, health and fitness, family and relationship. Then we can predict behaviour. More importantly, if we can organise our values in order of importance, in exactly the way we want it, we'll have an even better chance of creating a life by design.

I personally believe you should know what your top 3 to 5 values are in all areas of life. Personally, I have broken down my areas of life into 6 parts - spirituality, career and finance, personal development, relationship, health and fitness and family. Perhaps you want to break it up into 8 areas or 12 areas, it doesn't matter the principle is still exactly the same. I have 6 areas to mine and others have 8 areas broken down as spiritual and emotional, communicational and cultural, physical and health, intellectual and educational, recreation social, financial and wealth, professional and career and family and home, and some people have 12 areas.

Anyway, knowing your values is very important because then you can set goals, life purpose and make career decisions in alignment with your values. Just as Stephen R Covey's quote suggested above.

When your values are aligned with your goals, life purpose and career choices then that is what I call a marriage made in heaven.

We already know that values are what, is really important to you in a particular context, for example career or health and fitness.

So, what are values specifically?

They are usually short words or phrases that describe a state of being e.g. honesty, integrity, wisdom, vision, people, activities, wildlife, places, feelings, compassion, faith, decisiveness, generosity, fulfilment, passion, respect, love, trust, friendship, empathy, caring, truthfulness, good IQ, vocabulary, make a difference, help, peace, leave a legacy, contribution, fun, quietness, curiosity, discipline, detail, dynamic, diversity, education, wealth, persistent, determination, moderation, popular, cleanliness, accountability, reputation, responsibility, service to others, humble, god honouring, friendly, forgiveness, competitive, creative, analytical energetic, fair, joyful, patient, pride, proficiency, faithful, charming, uncompromising, wealthy, financially free, competent, fun-loving, hope, enthusiastic, cultured, organised, family, social, recreation, intellectual growth, fit & healthy, justice, kindness leadership, liberality, kindness, financially independent, leadership, independent, merit, motivational, numbers, order, organisation, originality, participation, challenge, freedom, teamwork, stability, money etc. The list is endless.

The challenge for most people is that your values are unconscious, meaning that they are not readily recognised compared to someone's attitude or beliefs.

Your core values are even more unconscious than you everyday values. So, the questions are how are values formed and what are the major sources of values?

What is the formation of values? According to the extensive research done by the Sociologist Morris Massey, who says that they are 4 major periods that a person goes through in terms of creating their core values and their personality formation.

This research is known as "The Massey's Developmental Period"

Here are the 4 different major periods:

SOURCE: *The People Puzzle*

1. 0 – 7 the Imprint Period - You are like a sponge taking it all in

2. 7 – 14 the Modelling Period – Who you worship at 10 you are at 40

3. 14 – 21 the Socialization Period – Time for rebellion

4. 21 – 35 the Business Persona we become – Formed by your first job

THE IMPRINT PERIOD

The Imprint Period, from birth to age 7, is the time when we are like sponges and we soak up everything around us and we store it. Literally, everything that goes on in our environment, you get all your basic programming from your Imprint Period. From the age of 2-5 your basic programming is completed.

This is the major reason why most therapeutic interventions usually go back to the Imprint Period to resolve traumatic childhoods because this is where your basic programming is stored regardless of whether you are aware of it consciously or not.

THE MODELLING PERIOD

This is a very significant period in children's development, from the age of 7 – 14 the child begins to consciously and unconsciously model basic behaviours of others around them.

I can clearly remember when I was about 9 years old. I was with my Dad, who had a peculiar walking style. And at the time I would be unconsciously mimicking my Dad's walk. Perhaps you too can recall memories of how you modelled adults during this period.

If you observe children closely with their parents, you will see generally that young girls are acting and behaving like their mothers, older sisters or grandmothers and the same goes for boys acting and behaving like their fathers, older brothers, friends, family members etc.

According to Massey our major values about life are picked up between 7 and 14. This will be largely due to where you were and what was happening in the world when you were, 7-14.

THE SOCIALIZATION PERIOD

This is the period where the child goes through a Socialization Period where social interaction begins with other human beings. This is where the young adult picks up relationships and social values. Ages 14 through 21, is called, the Socialization Period.

It is also the period where children try things out for the first time and a period where children are observed to be more rebellious.

I remembered growing up in Lagos, Nigeria and when my parents told me I couldn't and shouldn't do something. I often asked myself, "Why have they told me not to do it, without any proper explanation or information?" This then resulted in me getting curious that I ended up disobeying them just to find out myself. I was experimenting a lot during these periods and I questioned a lot of things that were going on in my environment during the Socialization Period.

Perhaps you too can recall how you were during this period of your development – What where you into, drugs, sex, dancing, Rock and Roll?

THE BUSINESS PERSONA WE BECOME

At age of 21, values formation is just about complete. At this point core values do not change unless there is a significant emotional experience. From the ages of 21 through to 35, this is where are personality is refined, challenged and cemented.

Largely dependent on your first job, the role you played, who your boss was and your colleagues. They will all influence you in some way, shape or form but as Massey has outlined your core values do not change unless there is a significant emotional event that happens to you.

WHAT ARE THE SOURCES OF VALUES?

Sources of values are influencers, which are things, people, places, events, circumstances and situations that have been directly or indirectly responsible for creating your core values. So, what are the influencers that create our core values? Where do the major values come from? They come from our environment.

You and I would have very different core values because of what was happening for you and I based on significant events that occurred in our environment during the tender ages of 7, 8, 9, 10, 11, 12, 13 and 14.

FAMILY

Family imposes values on you. Accept or reject them it still has an effect on you, especially during the Imprint Period from birth to 7 years old. Here you are simply a sponge soaking everything up in your environment. You're heavily influenced as a child by your family (mum, dad, brother, sister, uncles, aunties, nieces, nephews, grandma and grandpa, step-mum, step-dad, step-siblings, half-brothers, half-sisters and including all your extended family members) The degree of their influence would depend on how often you saw them and what role they played in your upbringing. Family plays a significant role in shaping who we eventually become.

Hence the saying, "The things you do not change, your children would end up inheriting from you." That is the imposing values we unconsciously and consciously in some cases pass onto our children and they end up doing the same for their children and the chain reaction goes on until we consciously changed it.

FRIENDS

After family, the next, major contributor, to creating our core values are friends. Ask yourself, "Which of your friends had a major impact on your life?" During the Socialization Period friends had a serious impact because here's where as teenager children start to model their friends. For those of us, who are parents with children you would see that during this period your children already establish who their hero would be, and they start to model them.

Friends create values beyond our wildest dreams – It has been long debated and postulated that the five or six closest friends you spend time with will determine your bank balance.

SCHOOL

School installs values (the teacher, the room set up, uniforms, discipline, the students and the attitude of the students being in school).

Also, school and teaching techniques will also determine your values. The question is doing you have choice at school? Did you have no choice in school? The school you went to, was it integrated as in (boys and girls together) or (just boys only) or (just girls only)? The teachers were they sexist or racist? All these factors will have an influence on your values for sure.

I remembered in my school, Hope High School, our teachers had the same rights as our parents to beat us and discipline us; as a matter of fact we were more scared of our teachers than our parents.

RELIGION

Church's values (not just what they taught but how they related to the people, to men and women and the roles that they were directed to have i.e. men work and the women stay at home taking care of the house and family)

My values in this area changed due to significant shifts in understanding and knowledge of religions as a whole. My father was originally a Christian by birth but to marry my mother he had to convert into a Muslim, which he did but he was never a practicing one. Growing up I was more influenced by my mother's religion and as a teenager she taught me to pray and fast as a Muslim, but I found it a bit rigid for me and restrictive. I did some soul searching and eventually converted and became a Christian and got baptised in a local church. After 4 years of service to the local church and attending services every Sunday without fail.

I found myself in the same scenario as a Muslim (rigid and restricted). That's when I decided to move to a more spiritual path of meditation and Universality. I love people and believe that they are no one religion that is the best way or the only way. In my opinion they are many ways to serve and connect with our Origin or Source (God).

Everyone has the birth-right to serve and worship God through whatever religion -Christianity, Islam, Hinduism, Buddhism, Sheik, Confucianism, Jehovah's Witnesses, Sikhism, Jainism, Shaivism, Sufism, Ayyavazhi, Vaishnavism, Zoroastrian, Arya Samaj, Tibetan Buddhism, Ajivika, Balinese Hinduism, Mahayana, Sarnaism, Syriac, Wahhabism, Madhyamaka, Unitarianism, Ahl al-Hadith, Smarta Tradition, Shaktism, Native American Church, Siddha Yoga, Indian Pentecostal Church.

According to some estimates, there are roughly 4,200 religions in the world. Your faith or belief system, religion, would definitely have an impact on your values just as mine did.

MEDIA

Media has an influence on our values – newspapers, advertising, radio channels and television.

The media has been a programming force for values from ages

7 to 21 now for generations. Take music for instance, how as that shape your values from generation to generation. The lyrics in music are programming the values of an entire generation. What genre of music are you into? Listen to and watch what kind of songs your children or child listens to and observe this from the ages of 14 to 21. You will be able to predict what their values will be when they grow up and become adults. The major outlet of media that is largely responsible for setting values is television.

Television is virtually in every household in the world even in so called, "Third–World Countries" Access to Television is becoming the norm and if you choose not to have one in this day and age then you are considered to be wired or an alien form outer space. T.V. has created the instant gratification syndrome. This is the result of the underlying current of television commercials or ads, as you might know them as, which is, you have a headache, take a painkiller and the problem disappears.

T.V. has created the belief, in our youngster and children that whatever it is that they want, they can have it now.

To limit the influence T.V. has on your children especially during the ages of 0 to 14. Parents have to be extra vigilant as to censor what they watch and how much of it they watch. This will then have a direct or indirect influence on what they decide to expose themselves to from ages 14 to 21.

OTHER SOURCES OF VALUES TO TAKE INTO CONSIDERATION ARE:

ECONOMY

Economics creates values – What was the economic environment you grow up in? Were your parents well off or not? What was their relationship with money? Where you as a child growing up able to afford whatever it is that you wanted?

GEOGRAPHY

Geographical areas help create values – Where you grow up, affects your values. Did you grow up in a, Third-World country, Nigeria, Kenya, Zimbabwe, or in an affluent Western-World country, UK, USA, Germany?

DIFFERENT AGE GROUPS

All generation today across the world have different values, based on significant experiences that happened when they were 7, 8, 9, 10, 11, 12, 13 or 14 years old. The most significant age is 10 years old. So, what happened, when you were 10 years old and now you are in your 100s, 90s, 80s, 70s, 60s, 50s, 40s, 30s, and 20s in your teens.

HISTORICAL EVENTS

For example, those who experience the Wars – World War 1 and World War 2 would definitely have a very different core value to those who have never been or experience a war before.

Now that you know what values are and how they are formed let's turn our attending to how you can discover what your values are in all areas of life.

HOW DO YOU DISCOVER YOUR VALUES?

The way to discover your values is through elicitation. This is an NLP process called, "Values Elicitation Exercise"

Follow the instruction below to begin eliciting your values now:

VALUES ELICITATION EXERCISE

This is a very simple process as you are only ever asking yourself one question repeated over and over again.

You will need to elicit your values in all areas of life like, career, relationships, family, health & fitness, personal growth and spirituality. But remember you only work with one area at a time. When you've finished with one area then move on to the next until you have fully completed eliciting all of your values in all areas of life.

Here's the magical question you ask:

"What's important to you about _(Insert the area you want to elicit here i.e. Career)_____ right now?"

Note: Only work with one area at a time!

If you are like most people you can consciously reveal around 3-5 values in rapid succession. By repeating the question, and demanding more answers, you will be able to reveal more values. Many times, in my coaching experience (with many clients from all walks of life) we have discovered that the values they discover the third or fourth time they ask this question are actually quite important on the values hierarchy. More about that later.

The goal here is to have at least 15 – 20 values for each areas of life you are working with.

Get yourself a notebook to write in and ask the above question. Once you have written down 3-5 or more values and you can't think of anymore then repeat the question:

"What else is important to you about _____ right now?"

Again, here try to come up with 3-5 more values then ask yourself the question again:

"And what else is important to you about _____ right now?"

Keep repeating this question until you have 15 – 20 values written down for Career for example. And it could be things like, Money, Freedom, Camaraderie, Challenge, Closing Deals and Creativity etc.

ORDER YOUR VALUES

The next phase of the exercise is to prioritize your values in order of importance to you. This is what is known as values hierarchy. Now don't get me wrong here, all values are important, but we have an order of importance for them unconsciously and here we want to make that order conscious.

The result is that you will end up with your top 3-5 values in all areas of life and this will proof very useful when you are going after jobs, careers, businesses or just finding your purpose in life.

Second step is to list out all the values you've elicited above. Now go ahead and number the values in order of importance to you from 1-15 or 1-20 depending on how many values you've elicited.

Ask yourself, "What's the most important values here in terms of my career mark that value as number 1. Then ask the question, "What's the next most important value? And follow this pattern of questioning until you have all the values numbered in order of importance to you.

If this doesn't work, then use a-b-c below:

    A. Of the above values, which is the most important to you?"

    B. Assuming you have [list values already chosen], is _____ or _____ more important to you?"

    C. Assuming you have [list values already chosen], if you couldn't have _____ but you could have _____, would that be OK?"

The a-b-c model is great as it allows you to play devil's advocate by comparing one value against another and checking which one is more important to you. E.g. sticking with the Career example let's say you had written down these values from the initial elicitation exercise, Money, Freedom, Camaraderie, Challenge and Creativity. You could start with Money and say, "Is Money more important than Freedom, or is Money more important than Camaraderie and continue in that vein until decide if Money is your number 1 or not. Then start with Freedom and do the same by comparing it against all other values written down.

WRITE DOWN YOUR TO 3-5 VALUES

The third and final phase is to now write down your top 3 to 5 values for Career. Then check your list one more time and make sure you are happy with it. Ask yourself, "Does it look okay or would you like to make any modifications?"

Once you are happy with it then you are done.

Now you can move onto another area of life in your wheel of life and repeat the 3 phases for each one of your 6, 8 or 12 of areas of life that you have decided to work with.

HOW DO YOU USE YOUR VALUES?

Now you know what your values are you can readily predict your own behaviour as you now know why you do what you do and why it's important to you.

Let's say John is looking for a new job and is values in the context of career are as follows: 1. Results 2. Integrity 3. Success 4. Relationship 5. Money. Now that he knows what's important to him, he should now be looking for a company that shares similar values at least 3 out of 5 values. You see a company that is committed to Results and Integrity and realises that their overall Success depends on their ability to maintain team and customer Relationships at a high level, as well as making Profits, which allows them to compensate their team generously. This type of company will definitely appeal to John more than one that doesn't meet his values.

When you know what your values are, you are more in control of your life and rather than doing things by default you are doing things by design.

Another way of attributing values is by understanding what human needs drives you as a person. Let's talk about human needs.

HUMAN NEEDS

If you are going to explore what human needs are then we need to mention Abraham Maslow.

Abraham Maslow has been considered the Father of Humanistic Psychology. Maslow's theory is based on the notion that experience is the primary phenomenon in the study of human learning and behaviour. He is famous for proposing that human motivation is based on a hierarchy of needs.

Let's talk about those needs because those needs are just human values in my opinion.

MASLOW'S HIERACHY OF NEEDS

PHYSIOLOGICAL NEEDS

They consist of needs for oxygen, food, water, and a relatively constant body temperature. They are the strongest needs because if a person were deprived of all needs, the physiological ones would come first in the person's search for satisfaction. We need these for basic survival. Maslow's theory said that you need to satisfy first the basic needs like Physiological needs and Safety needs, to get motivation to truly attain the higher-level needs like social needs and esteem.

SAFETY NEEDS

When all physiological needs are satisfied and no longer dominating our thoughts and behaviours, we progress to safety needs. A person's attention turns to safety and security for himself/ herself to be free from the threat of physical and emotional harm.

Such needs might be fulfilled by:

- Living in a safe area
- Medical insurance
- Job security
- Financial reserves

These include the need for security. We often have little awareness of these, except in times of emergency &

disorganization in social structure (war time, terrorist acts, domestic violence, natural disasters). Maslow's hierarchy said that, if a person feels that he or she is in harm's way, higher needs would not be attained that quickly.

BELONGINGNESS & LOVE NEEDS

When a person has attained the lower level like Physiological and Safety needs, higher level needs become important, the first of which are social needs. Social needs are those related to interaction with other people like:

- Need for friends
- Need for belonging
- Need to give and receive love

When safety and physiological needs are met, we desire, to be loved by others and to belong. Maslow states that people seek to overcome feelings of loneliness & alienation. This involves both giving & receiving love, affection & the sense of belonging (family, friends, social groups).

ESTEEM NEEDS

After the first 3 classes of needs are met, the needs for esteem can become dominant. These involve needs for both self-esteem & for the esteem a person gets from others. Esteem needs may be classified as internal or external. Self-respect and achievement are some examples of Internal esteem needs. Social status and recognition are some examples of External esteem needs. Some esteem needs are:

- Self-respect

- Achievement
- Attention
- Recognition
- Reputation

Humans have a need for a stable, firmly based, high level of self-respect, & respect from others.

When these needs are satisfied, the person feels self-confident & valuable as a person in the world. When these needs are frustrated, the person feels inferior, weak, helpless & worthless.

SELF-ACTUALIZATION NEEDS

When all of the foregoing needs are satisfied, then and only then are the needs for self-actualization activated. The last necessity is the Self Actualization or Fulfilment Needs. This includes purposed, personal growth, and the full realization of one's potentials. This is the point where people start becoming fully functional, acting purely on their own volition, and having a healthy personality.

Maslow describes self-actualization as a person's need to be & do that which the person was "born to do." "A musician must make music, an artist must paint, and a poet must write."

These needs make themselves felt in signs of restlessness (person feels edgy, tense, lacking something, restless.)

The person must be true to his or her own nature, be what you are meant to be.

Maslow believed that very few people reach the state of self-actualization. Although we all have the need to move toward the goal of reaching our full potential, other needs may get in the way.

Misconceptions about Maslow's Hierarchy of Needs

Maslow himself agreed that his 5-level need hierarchy oversimplifies the relationship between needs & behaviour. The order of needs makes sense for most of us, though there may be some notable exceptions (e.g., some people need to satisfy their needs for self-esteem & respect before they can enter a love relationship).

We may so desire fulfilling a need that we sacrifice others below it. For example, a person with a passion for acting might sacrifice his or her hunger, which is one of physiological needs, to pursue a career in acting even though the payment is barely enough and struggling to live while trying to make a name for themselves in the business.

Maslow was interested in studying people who are psychologically healthy. These were people who had become self-actualized. He interviewed these people to see how they were able to satisfy all the needs on the hierarchy. He conducted what he called a "holistic analysis" in which he sought general impressions from his efforts to understand these people in depth.

What is a self-actualized person like? They tend to accept themselves for what they are. They freely admit their weaknesses but do make attempts to improve.

They don't worry excessively over the mistakes they have made, but instead focus on improving.

They respect & feel good about themselves. However, this self-love is healthy and not narcissistic.

They are less restricted by cultural norms than the average person. They feel free to express their desires, even if contrary to the popular view. These people have frequent peak experiences, in which time and place are transcended, anxieties are lost, and a unity of self with the universe is obtained - birth of a child, marriage, deciding to go to school.

Another famous individual (Anthony Robbins) took the work of Maslow and improved upon it. Anthony Robbins is a world-renowned change specialist and widely known for being the coach to the stars (Top Actors and Actresses), the celebrities of this world. Tony, as he likes to be called has been listed among the top 50 most influential individuals on the planet.

He came up with, "The 6 Human Needs" This has been widely taught in many seminars, events, workshops across the globe. It's very similar to Abraham Maslow's Hierarchy of Needs but perhaps maybe better simplified – I'll let you be the judge of that.

According to Tony Robbins, there are six human needs – fundamental drivers if you will, remember values are what drives your behaviour, within each one of us. That compels us forward in a quest to experience a life of meaning.

He believes, and I agree that human needs psychology provides an answer to the age-old question, "Why do human beings do the things they do?" How is that one person can kill an innocent person in an instance and not bat an eyelid, just for the sheer pleasure of it? How is that another person is able to endure serious pain and sacrifice their own life, so they could safe another? What created a Steve Jobs or a Nelson Mandela or a Hitler or Mahatma Ghandi or a Mother Theresa?

No matter who you are in the world, or what you do, there's a common force that's driving and shaping all our emotions and actions. It determines the quality of our lives, and ultimately, what we end up creating in it.

This universal driving force is what Tony calls, "Human Needs."

Regardless of who we are our backgrounds, our professions, our religion, race, sex or creed. You, me and everyone else on this planet, are all driven by this universal force, day after day, to fulfil primal needs that have been encoded into our nervous systems over centuries. Although each of us is a unique beautiful soul but as human beings we are all wired the same.

Tony divides the human needs into two main categories: The Four Primal Needs and The Two Spiritual Needs. Let's look at this in more detail – And what I want you to do as you are reading about each of the six human needs is to start to identify which human needs is driving you right now and more importantly how are you meeting these needs in your life right now.

This will be a worthwhile exercise to engage in, so spend some time exploring this section.

TONY ROBBINS'S SIX HUMAN NEEDS

THE FOUR PRIMAL NEEDS

CERTAINTY

It doesn't take a brain surgeon to know that everyone wants stability and security in their lives. Their necessities are a must for their survival. Things like food, shelter, and other material resources. When people cannot control their physical circumstances, they may seek certainty through a state of mind (such as religious faith or a positive outlook).

Here are some ways, negative and positive, in which you could be meeting this need right now:

- Stuck in a comfort zone
- Developing a routine
- Avoidance of situations or people
- Making a plan
- Controlling situations, circumstances or people
- Procrastination, never getting anything done
- Facts and figures, fact findings and gathering proof or evidence
- Food – emotional eating disorders or just comfort eating
- Learned helplessness – depressed or anxious all the time
- Smoking, drugs, alcohol
- Faith, belief, religion (God)

How are you meeting your need for certainty right now?

UNCERTAINTY/VARIETY

Here is the paradox, in as much as we want certainty we also need variety, uncertainty. Imagine if you knew absolutely everything that is going to happen in your life how would you feel about that? I'm guessing for most people life would be completely boring and un-entertaining.

People have a need to change their state, to exercise their body and emotions. Therefore, they seek variety through a number of means to stimulate themselves. A change of home or scenery get involved in physical activities, mood swings, entertainment, food etc.

Here are some ways (negative and positive) in which you could be meeting this need right now:

- Smoking, drugs or alcohol
- Creating drama – drama queen or king
- New relationship/s
- New job
- New location
- Learn something
- Stimulating conversation (universe, god or energy)
- Crime
- All types of sports
- Adrenaline rush – extreme sports (F1, diving, fire-walking or glass walking)

How are you meeting your need for uncertainty/variety right now?

SIGNIFICANCE

This is a very strong driver as in everyone needs to feel special ad important in some way shape or form. People will seek significance through obtaining recognition from others or from themselves. When people feel insignificant, they may make themselves feel significant by getting angry or annoyed. They may also meet their needs paradoxically, by having others recognise the significance of their insignificance or the size and complexity of their problems. It's important to remember that for most people, helplessness is real power

Here are some ways, negative and positive, in which you could be meeting this need right now:

- Tear others down to make yourself feel important
- Violence, crime – carrying a knife or a gun
- Negative identity for self and others
- Material possessions
- Accomplishments, accolades, trophies and awards
- Style and look - wearing brand name clothing
- Superior knowledge
- Unique abilities
- Amplification – over exaggerating, blowing things out of context
- Winning attitude
- Martyrdom

How are you meeting your need for significance right now?

CONNECTION & LOVE

Humans need to feel connected with something or someone. A person, an ideal, a cause, a value, a habit or just a sense of belonging or identity. Connection may take on many forms, love, engagement, a heated debate or an aggressive interaction such us arguing with someone. It is widely documented that we settle mainly for the connections rather than the love. This is also a paradox as in we want to connect with others and be loved in our relationships but then we don't want to lose a sense of self. So, we seek to be significant and stand out from the crowd. Then when you've found yourself and you are being yourself then you have this urge to connect with others again. To put it mildly we are screwed we have issues.

Here are some ways, negative and positive, in which you could be meeting this need right now:

- Sympathy via sickness
- Crime – being part of a gang culture
- Smoking, drugs or alcohol (originally started out because you wanted to fit in and be part of the in crowd)
- Compliance – following the rules or party line
- Intimacy – in to me you see
- Spirituality – meditation or mindfulness groups
- Networking groups, business groups – BNI or clubs - for example golf memberships
- Pets
- Nature
- Leading and inspiring others

How are you meeting your need for connection and love right

now?

With regards to the four primal needs above there is no conscious effort required or necessary, our will to satisfy them is automatic.

THE TWO SPIRITUAL NEEDS

GROWTH

Everything in the universe is either, growing or dying, creating or disintegrating, there is no other option or alternative. People are not spiritually satisfied unless their capacities are expanding –And your human spirit is always for fuller expansion and expression. Hence why not matter what we achieve, we all have an innate desire for increase – and a desire is the yarning possibilities within you that is wanting to express itself through you.

Growth is achieved when the search for uncertainty/variety comes from the stability of certainty.

How are you meeting your need for growth right now?

CONTRIBUTION

No man or woman is an island alone; and no man or woman can become wealth or acquire any significant wealth on their own, they need other people to participate. It's a fact that we cannot survive without others contributing to us in some way. Take for instance babies – No babies grew up on their own.

I wrote a quote in my first book, "Empower Yourself with 7 Natural Laws" and the quote is,

"People make people and people break people but you still need people around you!"

Contribution is achieved through becoming significant (Self-actualised) in comparison to others and then connecting with others to lead and inspire them to do the same.

It's only by meeting the spiritual needs that you will experience sustainable joy and happiness vs. just monetary pleasures.

People find a way to meet these needs/values in positive, negative, or neutral ways, but everyone finds a way to meet them in some way.

Any activity, action, or emotion that fulfils at least three needs/values at a high level becomes, in effect, an addiction. Likewise, people have positive, negative, and neutral addictions.

The whole purpose here is to assess how you are currently meeting these needs/values. There is always a way to fulfil a need/value; the skill lies in finding a sustainable way to fulfil it, and in a way that gives you more pleasure than pain but does not violate the rights of others.

Now that you know what your values are, and you understand your human needs – Let's talk about evaluation.

WHAT IS EVALUATION?

Evaluation is to question things – When you ask yourself the right questions it literally directs your focus and what you focus on you feel. Feelings are emotions and emotion is life.

The question is what type of questions are you asking yourself on a daily, weekly or monthly basis?

Are you asking questions that keep you playing small, stuck, stagnate, feeling crap about yourself or are you asking questions that allow you to play a bigger role and make bigger impacts, or questions that allow you to solve challenges or problems?

If you think of your brain as a Google Search Engine - Now if you ask Google for any question it will provide you with the right answers, right? So, will your brain too, just like Google but if you ask a shitty question then it will provide you with a shitty answer. Let's explore the types of questions to avoid asking your Google brain and the type of questions to actually ask your Google brain.

QUESTIONS TO AVOID ASKING YOUR GOOGLE BRAIN:

- Why doesn't anything go right for me?
- Why am I so stupid?
- Why does it always happen to me?
- How come I'm the one you always end up getting cheated on?
- Why must I give up my position for him/her or them?
- Why can't I get it, others are getting it apart from me?

- What is wrong with me?
- Why I am so clumsy?
- Why I am fat?
- Why doesn't anybody love me or care about me?
- Why can't I find a man or a woman that can love me?
- How come I end up getting into the wrong relationships?
- Why am I cursed?
- What is wrong with the world and the people in it?

Suffice to say that all, "WHY?" questions should be banned and abolished as it just gets you whining all over yourself.

QUESTIONS TO DEFINITELY ASK YOUR GOOGLE BRAIN

- What am I happy about in my life right now?
- What am I excited about in my life right now?
- What have I given today?
- What's good about this situation right now?
- How can I reach more people today?
- How can I serve more people today?
- What did I learn today?
- What did I learn as result of what just happened?
- How can I use this challenge as a stepping-stone to allow me to grow from it?
- What am I proud about in my life right now?
- What am I grateful about in my life right now?
- What am I enjoying most in my life right now?
- How can I lose weight and enjoy the process alone the way?

- What am I committed to in my life right now?
- How can I show up every day expressing myself freely?
- How can I solve this problem right now?
- How can I invest in myself today for a better tomorrow?
- How can I make £100,000 (Insert whatever figure you want here) this year?
- How has today added to the quality of my life?
- How can I improve this situation?
- Who do I love and who loves me?
- How can I contribute more to society?
- How can I support my clients, customers, mentees, so they can create a bigger impact?

Come up with some of your own questions here…!

These questions will direct your focus in a positive way that will enhance the quality of your life.

SUMMARY: VALUES – WHAT DRIVES YOU?

- Values are what is important to you and what really is driving your behaviour.
- It's important to know what your top 3-5 values are in all areas of your life. This will allow you to create a life by design and not by default.
- Formation of value is explained by, "The Massey Developmental Periods"
- 0 – 7 the Imprint Period - You are like a sponge taking it all in
- 7 – 14 the Modelling Period – Who you worship at 10 you are at 40

- 14 – 21 the Socialization Period – Time for rebellion
- 21 – 35 the Business Persona we become – Formed by your first job
- Your family, friends, school, religion, media, economy, geography, the period or era you were born in and historical events are all sources of values.
- To elicit your values, use the elicitation question.
- "What's important to you about _(Insert the area you want to elicit here i.e. Career)_____ right now?"
- And repeat the question 2 to 3 more times as you elicit more values.
- Put your values into order of importance so you can establish which values are the most important to you.
- Human needs are human values, which ones are you driven by?
- Certainty, Uncertainty/Variety, Significance, Connection & Love these are your primal needs, which you always find a way to meet be it negatively, positively or neutrally.
- Your spiritual needs are Growth and Contribution, which are required if you are truly to create a fulfilling life.
- The only way to evaluate anything is to questions it. So the question is what type of questions are you asking yourself on a daily basis?
- Avoid, "WHY?" questions and ask more what, where, how, when questions.

"Determine what your values are, what human needs drives you, who you are and what you want to become before you decide what you want to give, be, do and have."

Tosin Ogunnusi

CHAPTER 3
SUCCESS – WHAT DO YOU WANT?

"Dream lofty dreams, and as you dream, so you shall become. Your VISION is the promise of what you shall one day BE; your IDEAL is the prophecy of what you shall at last UNVEIL.

The greatest achievement was at first, and for a time, a dream. The oak sleeps in the acorn; the bird waits in the egg; and in the highest vision of the soul, a waking angel stirs. Dreams are the seedlings of realities.

Your Circumstances may be uncongenial, but they shall not long remain so if you but perceive an ideal and strive to reach it.

You cannot travel WITHIN, and stand still WITHOUT."

James Allen

"Success is the manifestation of big, exciting, service-oriented goals"

In my experience society and the media as an erroneous view or a make-believe view of what success is. You see most of us are leading to believe that success is money, power, fame – The house you live in the car you drive and your current title at work etc. Now don't get me wrong there is nothing wrong with material wealth or wanting the best of things for yourself and your family. Just understand that, that is not success – These things are just by-products of success.

So, what is success?

The best definition that I have ever heard by Napoleon Hill about success is, *"Success is a progressive realisation of a worthy ideal."* Now what does that really mean? Let's break it down for you.

A worthy ideal is something that you and I have fallen in love with at all levels, spiritually, mentally and physically. It's something that you are truly passionate about – And as a result of pursuing your passion or dedicating yourself to your craft then the money, power, fame and material possessions will surely be yours.

Too many people are caught up in the hamster wheel of life, rat race trying so hard to chase after the money, power and fame to no avail.

The honest question to ask is, what is my "WHY" for doing what I do? Am I doing it just to make a buck or is this really what lights me up, gives my life meaning and purpose?

You see, the truth of the matter is you could be a beggar on a park bench with a clear vision of what you want to give, be, do, have and you believe whole-heartedly that you can achieve it – And go about taking small daily actions towards that vision - Then you are successful! That is true success!

Success is, knowing what you want and finding ways to get what you want period.

Let me ask you this, have you ever set a goal and not achieved it? Have you ever set a goal and achieved it?

I'm sure you will agree with me that the answer to both questions is a resounding, "YES!"

So, the real question is how do you set a goal so that you can consistently achieve it and become quote and quote successful?

This entire chapter on success is focused on giving you a clear and precise methodology for setting goals and achieving it.

Before I explain what this methodology is, here's a story about manifesting your Goal:

My ex-partner got pregnant in September 2008. She is about 5ft 7" tall, short bob like dark hair. She's a very smart cookie – Her nickname is "fix it lady" by her family! Just make sure, if you don't want something done then don't mention it to my ex-partner otherwise she's on it in a flash and it's done. She had a reputation for getting what she wants. I'm sure you someone like this in your circle perhaps that person is you?

Now, that she was pregnant she shared her thoughts and ideas with me. She said at the time, "Babes, I want to give birth to our baby naturally, this is my goal!" Considering she has never giving birth before this was our first child together.

She opted to have a home birth using a birth pool.

So, I said, "Wow, babes, that is wonderful and I'm sure you will – I mean coming from a very strong African background giving birth naturally was the only option our mothers had. There was no other form of delivery open to our parents in those days.

It's only in the last God knows how many years that other forms of giving birth has come about. I was told by a friend, of my ex-partner that the latest trend, is now about, "Being too, "Posh," to "Push" (for most of our celebrities and footballer's wives) and going in straight for a caesarean operation was more likely the option they would choose.

Early labour started on 10/06/09 Wednesday morning at which point ex-partner called her midwife and told her what was happening based on what she described was going on for her. She was told, her baby would be delivered by the end of the day – By the end of the day nothing had happened.

The contractions continued into Thursday (11/06/09), this time they were stronger and more frequent, but she was still only 2 centimetres dilated and her contractions were 4/5 minutes apart lasting about 1 minute. She was told that they needed to be 2/3 minutes apart lasting about the same time and be 4 centimetres dilated for her to be in full labour. Again, based on what was occurring she was told that there was no way she would have her baby on Thursday.

At about 2.30pm her midwife came to visit, she examined her, and nothing had changed

At 6.30pm two other midwives came to relieve the first

midwife. She was examined, and nothing had changed.

At 10.00pm two other midwives came to relieve the second pair of midwives. She was examined, and nothing had changed.

The pain was so unbearable for her that they allowed her into her birthing pool at about 10.30pm in the hope that this would help to alleviate some of the pain.

Four hours later, she had made some progress and was now 8 centimetres dilated but 2 hours after that she was examined again, at which point they detected a complication. The baby was back to back with the mother and his head was facing up instead of down. She had been breathing with the aid of a gas. The midwives only had two tanks with them of which she was on the last one. At this point my ex-partner was absolutely exhausted.

She had a decision to make and was given the following options:

This is what the midwife told her, "My dear am so sorry, I know you wanted to have a home birth and give birth to your baby naturally, but your cervix has not given way as we had hoped and we feel you need stronger pain killers to assist you further in delivering your baby. So, we need to go to the hospital and also bear in mind with the position of your baby being back to back you are looking at a possible C-section. So, what do you want to do?"

At this point her eyes welled up with tears and I looked at her helplessly as she held my hands really tightly. She replied by saying, "I am exhausted, I don't care how the baby comes out just get it out; I don't care if they have to cut me open!"

She agreed to go to hospital and an ambulance was called and we arrived at the hospital about 6.00am on a Friday morning of the 12th June 2009.

At 10.00am, she was examined, and nothing had changed from previous examination.

They gave her a pink tablet, pumped her with hormones and administered epidural all in preparation for a C-section.

At 12 noon, my ex-partner was now fully dilated but how was she going to now push her baby out naturally when she has been fully pumped up with an epidural, hormones and had been breathing with the aid of a gas, which makes you feel nauseous and fuzzy. She was exhausted, not to mention the complication of having her baby back to back and head facing up instead of down.

She asked the midwife at the hospital, "How long have I got before they take me in?"

She said, "An hour"

In that moment my ex-partner had a mind shift (you might call it a divine intervention). Her spirit was renewed she started to push as hard as she can, encouraged along by the midwife and myself.

She started shouting, "Yes, Yes, Yes, and saying to herself I can do this" – All the while strangling my hands in hers so tight that I thought my fingers were broken. She pushed so hard I thought she was going to explode. She looked like the, Michelin Man from the tyre ads on T.V. And at 1.10pm in the

afternoon on Friday 12th of June 2009 baby Leon was born –
Exactly on his due date. He weighed 8lb 1oz.

My ex-partner demonstrated very clearly to you how to keep
on, believing, even when everything around you seemed to be
telling you otherwise. She stayed true to her goal.

Now this story illustrates the 7 steps to creating long-lasting
success and by success I'm referring to a clear strategy for
achieving your goals. It also demonstrates why it is very
important for you to have a definite goal in mind that you are
striving for.

Before I outline the 7 steps let's explore the reasons why it is
important for you to have a goal in the first place.

WHAT IS THE PURPOSE OF HAVING A GOAL OR SETTING A GOAL?

There are many reasons why we as human beings you need a
goal in your life:

DIRECTION AND FOCUS

It is a known fact that setting goals and having a clear defined
goal that you want will give you a sense of direction and focus
in life.

Imagine a football game without goal posts and they are two
teams of 11 players each kicking around a round ball but with
no clear purpose or goal in mind. What would be the outcome
of the game?

There would be no purpose whatsoever for the game ever taking place as they would be no objective for it without any goal post because we wouldn't be able to determine which team has won or lost the game. So, without goal posts for the opposition team to score from the game of football would be absolutely pointless. The players will have no sense of direction or purpose.

Here's an instance for you, let's say you were travelling somewhere using the train. When you get to the train station the guy or lady behind the counter asks you, "Sir/Madam, where would you like to go today?" And your response was, "I don't know or nowhere?"

The ticket sales person would then respond by saying, "Sir/Madam, if you don't know where you are going, or you are going to nowhere then I'm afraid we don't have any tickets going to nowhere and if you don't know where you are going then I'm afraid I can't help you!"

So, if you are someone without a goal in life then you have no sense of direction or focus and you are merely drifting along and allowing situations and circumstances to drag you along through life aimless. This is why it is very important to know what you want and set clear defined goals to get what you want – In other words know in which direction of life you are heading in and have a laser focus on what you want.

AN EXPRESSION OF SELF

You need goals to express who you are – A wise man once told me that, "You and I and everyone on the planet is a

SPIRITUAL BEING, having a human experience. Therefore, you are an expression of spirit, meaning contrary to whatever you believe (The nucleus of your being is spiritual). Spirit is always for expansion and fuller expression of itself. All of nature expands and expresses itself in a greater way. Nature knows no failures and you are part of nature. Hence why having a well-defined goal that can allow you to express your true essence is vital.

It is often said, "It's not achieving the goal that's the big deal, it's who you become in the process of achieving your goal that's the big deal!"

CO-CREATION

Having goal and setting goals is a form of co-creation or manifestation. You are literally a co-creating machine because you are manifesting all the time.

Dissatisfaction with life is a healthy creative state of mind and when we look at history today, we can clearly see that it is this state of mind that has allowed us to invent new ways and come up with new ideas of how to improve things or do things in a different way. So a healthy dissatisfaction for the way your life is could be the catalyst for change.

For example: You would still be illumination your home with a wax candle or kerosene lamp if Thomas Edison had not created the light bulb because of his healthy dissatisfaction with the wax candle.

The wright brothers did the same when they created the first planes. Alexandra Graham Bell also invented the first telephones and now we have mobile phones that we can carry around with us everywhere we go.

When you become sufficiently dissatisfied with your life as it is, you will begin to think of ways to improve it – And that way begins with you deciding on a goal.

How are you living now? What are you doing in comparison to what you know you can do with the potential you possess? Keep asking yourself questions like these above and it will assist you in having a clear focus of what you really want in life.

Here's the thing, if you are not co-creating then you're disintegrating; in other words you are either living or dying period. In nature everything is contributing to the whole, otherwise it is eliminated.

HAPPINESS & PEACE OF MIND

Ultimately, you want to be fulfilled in life, right? What bring us that happiness and peace of mind? Before I answer that let me just be very clear that happiness and peace of mind are not goals but a by-product of achieving our goals.

Material things and money will not make you happy because they were not designed to make you happy. Awareness is the only thing, which can provide you with happiness and peace of mind. Material things and money were designed to make you comfortable.

I believe it was George B. Shaw that said, "It is a sin to be poor."

I completely agree with him. So, what is money?

MONEY (My Own Natural Energy Yield) is a reward received for services rendered.

Based on the definition above if you want more money then you must provide more service.

As human beings you are always seeking for increase. The desire for more is an innate ability that you were born with.

All human activities are based on the desire for increase. Hence why people are seeking for more food, more clothes, better homes, more luxury, better cars, more beauty, more knowledge, more pleasure, more experiences and more of life itself.

To have more, you have to give more – The law decrees, "Give and you shall receive." If you are not receiving much, you are not giving, and that is criminal.

It is well documented that for you to be truly happy and peaceful then you must be growing in some way and be contributing to humanity or society in some meaningful way as well. And, all of that starts by giving, remember: Life is Giving!!!

Now that you know the real purpose of setting or having a goal - And that "MONEY" is just your own natural energy yield, which is just a reward for services rendered. In other words, a reward for the value you bring or provide for others. You can now discover what 7 steps to creating long-lasting success are:

7 STEPS TO CREATING LONG-LASTING SUCCESS

1. SET YOUR GOALS

The first step is to take time out to set your goals every year. Remember you have one life, there are no trial runs here so live it. Reflect on your year to date and be really honest and candid with yourself here. Identify where you are now clarifying where you want to be the following year.

Here you need to engage your imagination with absolute clarity & belief that you can achieve what you set out to achieve.

> *"If a person advances confidently in the direction of their dream, and endeavors to live the life they have imagined, they will meet with success unexpected in common hours." Henry Thoreau*

Now it's your turn to set your goals, follow the goals setting instructions below:

GOALS SETTING INSTRUCTIONS

Write out 15 things that you really want, if you knew you could have anything that you wanted and you could ask for any amount of money, how much would you ask for a month? If you knew you could not fail what would you, give, be, do and have? What do you really want? If you need more space to write in then do this exercise on a separate piece of paper or better still buy a journal for this exercise and perform this exercise in it each year so you can keep it and review it each year.

1.

2.

3.

4.

5.

6.

7.

8.

9.

10.

11.

12.

13.

14.

15.

Now that you have written down your 15 goals, you need to prioritise your goals in the following order:

1. To prioritise your goals, you should put A, B, or C next to you goals. A being the most important goals to you and B being the next important goals to you and C your least important goals to you. By the end of this exercise you should have five A goals, five B goals and five C goals.
2. Here you are going to further prioritise your goals by numbering them. Look through your goals list within each section (A, B, C) and determine which one is most important to you. Take A section for example; insert 1 for the most important goal to you, 2 for the next important goal to you, 3 for the next important goal to you, 4 for the next important goal to you and finally, 5 for the least important goal to you. You need to repeat this exercise for sections B and C.
3. Now we are ready to proceed. The whole point of that exercise was to find your number 1 goal that is the A1 goal. On the next blank page you are going to expand on your A1 goal. All the other goals are equally important and what we have found is when people really focus on their number A1 that is the most important to them, then the other goals are just stepping stones along the way to achieving your A1 goal.

EXPAND YOUR A1 GOAL:

Here are some very important pointers to help you expand on your A1 goal:

1. Make simple sentences, write it in the present tense or past tense, as if it was already happening e.g. You will not write: "I would like to be more assertive". You would write: "I am an assertive person". Another example: You will not write: "I wish to live in a three-bedroom house with a big garden". You will write: " I am living in a three bedroom house with a big garden".
2. You will state it in the positive and add a lot of images and feelings to your writing as if it were already true.
3. Set a date and time that you will achieve this goal.

Here is a sample expansion of an A1 goal I created in January 2002 when I first did this exercise:

Oluwatosin Ogunnusi   **31st December 2003**

I am so happy and grateful now that I am a personal development coach, running various seminars around the world. Public Speaking is now a big part of my life, I am constantly speaking at seminars, functions, birthday, clubs, family dos, charity functions, and reunions and at social events. I have a great command of the English language coupled with a reservoir of words or vocabularies that encaptures, intrigues, encourages, inspires and engage my audience. I love and genuinely care for the people I talk to and this attribute always comes across in all my interactions. I am simply the BEST, trained by the BEST and taught the BEST to be the BEST!!!

When I started writing this book I looked back at this and I can honestly say that I have achieved everything that I set out to achieve and much more.

Here's another example of an expanded A1 goal:

Oluwatosin Ogunnusi   **31st December 2026**

I am so happy and grateful now that Mpowerment s.r.o. is earning £1.7 Million pounds in revenue every year. We have sold 800 Affiliate schemes to Corporate Clients, Coaches, Trainers and individuals to date. Time 2 Break Free Bootcamp (T2BFB) is the number 1 Teambuilding event for Companies not only in the UK but Internationally too. It is now generating a participative audience of 1000+ delegates at each event. The events are held at great locations like (The Excel Centre in Docklands). A minimum of 4000 delegates go through our T2BFB events every year i.e. over 1000 delegates per event. These individuals are now living the life they desire by attending our extraordinary seminar. Their lives have been transformed from ordinary people into extraordinary leaders within their teams. Work performances, KPI's, NPS scores and company bottom line profits have been improved dramatically. Numerous companies have won awards as a result of attending our T2BFB. It is a real joy and a blessing to be supported in all areas of life by the universe on this great quest of improving the world we live in one company and one team at a time. We are internally grateful to be a part of Gods work and one of God's instruments of light. Thank you Father – It is done just as it is written.

2. UNDERSTAND YOUR GOAL

The second step is to understand the "Why" behind your goals. What are the reasons why you want to achieve this A1 goal? Remember every goal in life must have a clear definite purpose. You can't just want more money, why do you want more money? To get married, buy a new house or a new car?

When you fully understand why you want what you what then you create the fuel to keep on going when obstacles show up and I promise you they will show up.

3. COMMIT TO YOUR GOAL

Once you've set your goal and you understand your reasons for wanting it then it's time to commit to it fully and whole-heartedly.

Ask yourself what resources do I have in my possession right now to accomplish or start working towards this goal right now?

Start taking immediate action with what you've got right now in this moment. Now you might be asking, "Tosin what have I got right now to begin working with that will allow me to achieve my goal?

Great question I thought you'll never ask? You have your imagination, which is known as the greatest nation in the world. Now that you have used your imagination to create your A1 goal, you are now going to use it to plant your goal into your subconscious mind (Your whole physical body). By your body, I mean your 50 Trillion cells (which is what your entire body is made of). It is also a known fact that every single cell in your body is ease dropping on your daily thoughts. Plus your subconscious mind cannot tell or differentiate between what is real or just imagined.

So, knowing this very vital fact you can support your mind and brain by creating brain cells for what you want and commit to it by installing it into your body. You do this through the art of visualization.

Here are some instructions for committing to your A1 goal:

1. Now you will need to make a recording of your A1 goal on a CD or audio programme on your computer. This will be in your own voice.
2. You will make a declaration to yourself on the CD or audio programme to listen to your A1 goal daily (first thing in the morning and the last thing before you go to bed) for 90 days.
3. Make sure you let yourself relax fully before you begin to listen to your recoding. This is very important.
4. Let yourself feel yourself already in possession of your goal.
5. Talk, walk, feel, taste, smell, see and act like you already have your goal in physical form.
6. Create a dream board or dream wall where you represent your goals with pictures of what you want; either you visit your goals and take pictures of cars and houses that you like or want, or you cut out images from magazines to represent your goals. Pictures and images speak 1000 words.

This commitment to your goal is a very powerful one. One that is omitted by most people, the mental rehearsal is equally as important as the physical actions we take if not more. Most people struggle with mental aspect of creating their goals.

The creation process happens as follows:

1. Your brain and mind are engaged in the idea, or ideal that you want that is your CONSCIOUS MIND involved with the image of your goal.
2. Your body (your cells) learn about your goals from your brain and mind through repetition (daily visualization) of your goal. This is your SUB-CONSCIOUS MIND emotionally involved with your goal.
3. Because of these two stages of creation, which is known as the MENTAL SIDE you engage the UNIVERSAL MIND, which is the MIND of every individual on the planet. This is also called, "THE UNIVERSAL INTELLIGENCE. When the image of your goal is properly planted in your sub-conscious mind, the image is not only automatically expressed through your body in vibration or actions, that image affects everything in the universe that is in direct harmonious vibration with it. This is how the, "LAW OF ATTRACTION" works.
4. The image in your conscious mind that is properly and firmly planted into your sub-conscious mind sets in motion a force to attract into your life all that is in harmony with it – And as you attract the image must affect or be expressed through your physical body (In other words you take ACTION) as a direct result of the attraction. This then causes the final act in the

creation process (The physical manifestation of your goal).

THE POWER AND ORDER OF VISUALIZATION

"The exercise of the visualizing faculty keeps your mind in order and attracts to you the things you need to make life more enjoyable, in an orderly way.

If you train yourself in the practice of deliberately picturing your desire and carefully examining your picture, you will soon find that your thoughts and desires proceed in a more orderly procession than ever before.

Having reached a state of ordered mentality, you are no longer in a constant state of mental hurry. 'Hurry' is 'Fear', and consequently destructive.

In other words, when your understanding grasps the power to visualize your heart's desire and hold it with your will, it attracts to you all things requisite to the fulfillment of that picture, by the harmonious vibrations of the law of attraction.

You realize that since ORDER is HEAVEN'S first law, and visualization places things in their natural order, then it must be a heavenly thing to visualize.

Everyone visualizes whether, they know it or not. Visualizing is the great secret of SUCCESS.

The conscious use of this great power attracts to you multiplied resources, intensifies your wisdom, and enables you to make use of advantages which you formerly failed to recognize."

Genevieve Behrend "Your Invisible Power"

4. CONTEMPLATE ON YOUR GOAL

Contemplating on your goal allows you to cultivate your mind and keep firmly focused on your goal. Remember where focus goes, energy flows.

> *"The only thing that can, grow is the thing you give energy to." Ralph Waldo Emerson*

When you become totally obsessed with your goal by committing to it fully and visualizing it at least once every day. Three things will occur:

1. The image of your goal becomes more crystalized and you begin to add all of the missing parts until you can see it clearly in your minds eyes as you can see the people and things around you.
2. You put yourself in the vibration you must be in to attract what you need and require fulfilling your goal.

3. Your self-image becomes comfortable and familiar with your goal – Meaning you create the experience well in advance of having the goal before it actually happens.

After, contemplation of your A1 goal makes, sure you re-write your image, in detail. Remembering that your goal is not something you going to get, it is something you already have INTELLECTUALLY and EMOTIONALLY.

It is only a matter of time before you have it PHYSICALLY created in your hands or your environment. Contemplating on your goal gives it energy.

As you re-write your daily contemplations be open to other subtle possibilities that perhaps haven't yet considered. Pay close attention to your intuition and the images and thoughts that you are receiving during this period. The irony is to know and believe in what you want, focus only on that, but then don't be so attached to the outcome that you are rigid and unbending. It's important to be open to other possibilities here.

The universe works in mysterious way and sometimes you want something to happen in a particular way, but the universe brings it about a whole different way.

Refer back to the story of my ex-partner above and this section will make perfect sense to you. If you remembered her goal was to give birth to our first son Leon naturally.

She didn't want to go to hospital and opted for a home birth instead but what happened next was not what she was expecting at all. In the end she had to be open to going to the hospital and accepting other possibilities just to keep her baby alive. She delivered her baby naturally after 3 days labor in the hospital.

It didn't happen exactly how she planned it to, but her goal was meant.

5. EVALUATE YOUR GOAL

Most people do not establish why they want what it is they want therefore when challenges show up they fall flat on their faces. Therefore, it is critically important to follow the second step by knowing the reason/s why you want your goal. This way when challenges happen which they will then you can fall flat on your back and in the words of Les Brown, "If you can see up then you can get up!"

Challenges, problems, frustrations, delays, distractions, failures, naysayers, obstacles, barriers, huddles, surprises and a host of things that can and will go wrong in the pursuit of your goals is an inevitable part of achieving any worth-while goal.

The trick is to ask yourself the right questions to make it happen, get yourself out of the situation you are in, find another alternative to the one you are using etc.

Remember questions direct your focus.

So when you ask "why" questions, it puts you in more of a negative state...a victim way of thinking i.e.," Why me?" Instead ask empowering questions like, "What can I do now to change this?" "What is this problem trying to teach me?"

"Who do I know that can help or support me in getting my outcome?"

Please refer to Chapter 2 on Values and read the section on Evaluation.

6. SURRENDER TO YOUR GOAL

Surrendering to your goal is a deep understanding that your goal has already happened regardless of how things may appear in your physical environment.

You already have your goal on the spiritual and intellectual levels of creation. Give thanks, gratitude and appreciation for it, enjoy it, and act as if you have it already because you do.

Understand, it is only a period of time until you can touch it with your physical body or enjoy it on the physical level, or until you can show it to someone else on the physical plane. You can already congruently share it with people around you on the other two levels through words and feelings.

Throughout history countless men and women had achieved great things because they had surrendered to their goals meaning they had an "UNSHAKABLE BELIEF" No one and nothing could disturb nor destroy their BELIEF that they were going to achieve what they had set out to achieve. People like Mother Theresa, Nelson Mandela, Steve Jobs, Walter Disney, James Dyson, Thomas Edison, Colonel Sanders, Margret Thatcher, Opera Winfrey, Portia Nelson just to mention a few.

These people above have found themselves in situations,

which appeared devastating, some of them lost fortunes, loved ones and some had to battle great physical problems, but they never appeared to waiver and somehow, there was an "INNER-KNOWING" that nothing could stop them in achieving their goals.

Similarly, to the story above about my ex-partner giving birth to our son Leon, all of the appearance of things pointed to her having a C-section due to the complications but somehow she believed she was going to give birth to her baby naturally and that is what she did.

7. STICK TO YOUR GOAL

Any meaningful goals take time to manifest. So, the question is, "How much time do you give yourself to reach your goal?

This is a very common question and as far as I'm aware no one has ever developed the awareness of how long it takes for a non-physical seed like ideas, goals, dreams, vision or desires to manifest in physical form. Therefore, you and I must guess at how much time we give ourselves for achieving our goals.

Northcote Parkinson's Law comes into play here:

"Work expands to fill the time allotted for it."

Now if the day that you have chosen arrives and you have not yet reached you goal, or there are no visible signs that you will ever reach your goal. Do not despair, it only means you chose the wrong time and date. Give yourself more time and keep going.

Remember also to be honest with yourself here did you follow through on the actions? And if you didn't that's okay, just do it and keep following through.

You see spirit or universal intelligence works in your world from the outside in through attraction, and from the inside out through action. It always expresses itself perfectly every time. The impaction only comes from your individual or collective way of thinking and acting.

Be 100% guaranteed that the universal intelligence will always take care of the 'ATTRACTION.' You on the other hand must take full responsibility for the ACTION.

Never change the goal, change the time and date, change the plan but always keep focused on the goal until you achieve it.

"Any idea that is held in the mind, that is emphasized, that is FEARED or REVERED will begin AT ONCE to cloth itself in the most convenient and appropriate form that is available."

Andrew Carnegie — As given to Napoleon Hill

SUMMARY: SUCCESS – WHAT DO YOU WANT?

- Success is a progressive realisation of a worthy ideal
- A worthy ideal is something that you and I have fallen in love with at all levels, spiritually, mentally and physically.
- Why is it important to have goal? You need goals for a sense of direction and focus, an outlet to express yourself, for creation and being part of life's flow and for happiness and peace of mind.
- How do you set and achieve goals on a consistent basis? You follow the 7 steps to creating long-lasting S.U.C.C.E.S.S.
- SETTING – The first step is to set your goals, decide with clarity what it is that you really want. Here use your imagination. Follow the goal setting exercise to come up with your A1 goal then expand on it an write it down in the present or past tense as if you already have it now.
- UNDERSTANDING – The second step is to understand why you want your goal. Remember reasons come first and answers come second. Knowing your reason why would help you stay the course and ultimately get you to be consistent and persistent in pursuit of your goal.
- COMMITTING – The third step is to commit to your goal by making a public or private declaration to yourself and others that you will visualise, read, write, listen to your goals daily for 90 days and beyond. Remember to record your goal in your own voice. It's vital that you here yourself speaking to yourself about

your goal. Beyond the mental rehearsal start taking immediate action with what you already have to get what you want.

- CONTEMPLATING – The fourth step is to contemplate on your goal. You must become obsessed with your goal think about it daily by reflecting on what is working and what is not working. This will give your goal energy so it can grow.
- EVALUATING – The fifth step is to evaluate your goal and when things don't go according to plan… Ask yourself the right can of questions that will allow you to shift your focus in a positive way.
- SURRENDERING – The sixth step is to surrender to your goal. Completely let go and let Universal Intelligence (GOD) intervene. Let the universe take care of the how (ATTRACTION) and you follow through by taking care of your thinking process in understanding the creative process and taking appropriate (ACTION) accordingly. The deciding factor is here is your unshakable belief that you already have in your possession what you are want.
- STICKING – The seventh and final step is to stick to your goal like glue. This is the magic formula – Never change your goal, change the time and date, change your approach, change destinations, change many other variables but stick with your goal until you have achieved it. I call this your, 'STICK-ABILITY'

"Desire is the effort of the unexpressed possibility within you, attempting to express itself through you in physical form."

Wallace D. Wattles

"If you want a thing bad enough, to go out and fight for it; work day and night for it, Give up your time, your peace and your sleep for it, If only desire of it, makes you quite mad enough never to tire of it, Makes you hold all things tawdry and cheap for it, If life seems all empty and useless without it, And all that you scheme and you dream is about it. If gladly you'll sweat for it, fret for it, plan for it Lose all your terror of God or man for it, If you'll simply go after that thing that you want, With all your capacity, strength and sagacity Faith hope and confidence, stern pertinacity, If neither cold poverty, famished and gaunt, Nor sickness, nor pain of body and brain Can turn you away from the thing that you want, If dogged and grim you besiege and beset it. You'll get it."
Berton Braley

CHAPTER 4
EMOTIONS – WHAT'S HOLDING YOU BACK?

"If you are depressed you are living in the PAST. If you are anxious you are living in the future. If you are at peace you are living in the present. The key is to express your emotions in every given moment."

Tosin Ogunnusi

What is an emotion? An emotion is a strong internal feeling derived from one's circumstances, mood or relationship with others.

Your internal state, feeling, mood or emotion, is directly link to your internal processing, thinking strategies, and your external behaviour, your body and the way in which you use your body i.e. posture.

It is said that at any given time or moment your body reflects or expresses your emotional state. It has to it doesn't know any other way to react.

This phenomenon can be clearly observed when someone is angry, happy, sad or fearful. Take the instance someone who is angry for example, his/her anger is a combination of sensations, interpretations (values and beliefs they hold) and behaviour they display to express that anger.

Your daily emotions are directly linked to behaviours, eternal behaviours.

Your emotions are also directly connected to physical sensations, as in you can describe your anger in detail. I am angry could be a tightening of the stomach muscles, which creates tension in your skin and an opening of the lungs.

Your emotions are directly linked to an interpretation, based on your values and beliefs, of your experience. For example: The physical sensations, described above, could be, perceived, by others, as fear, nervousness or rage.

This chapter is about how to manage your emotional states better rather than having your emotional states manage you.

You experience daily a range of emotions both negative and positive here are some the emotions you experience daily:

POSITVIE EMOTIONS

Love, joy, happiness, laughter, excitement, bliss, euphoria, confidence, strength, powerful, assertive, certainty, energised, relaxed, calm, patience, peacefulness, mindfulness, awareness, satisfaction, fairness, and uplifted, just to mention a few.

NEGATIVE EMOTIONS

Anger, sadness, fear, guilt, shame, conflict, regret, control, disgust, disappointment, hate, stress, revenge, bitterness, jealousy, envy, boredom, depression, anxiety, frustration, irritation and procrastination, just to mention a few.

A lot of research has been done and linking our emotions to overall wellbeing. If your daily vibrational energy is more positive than negative, then you say you are healthy but if your vibrational energy is more negative than positive then you say you are unhealthy or not feeling well.

I'm not going to focus on the various researches done here in this book. I will leave you to do your own research in this area. As a quick source of reference, you can check out my good friend, Dr Richard Moat the Mind-Body Expert, who spent 17 years researching this very topic after he lost his dad to cancer. Louise Hay the author of, "You Can Heal Your Life" has focused her life's work in this area. Famous for her affirmations for healing your body and the amazing Susan Jeffers, who wrote the book, "Feel the Fear and Do It Anyway".

Start you research about the impact of emotions and the role it plays in your life with these 3 incredible souls. This research is not just limited to this 3 there are numerous researches out there for you to explore. My personal belief is our emotions play a big part in our overall wellbeing.

My goal in this book is to outline some of the role these negative emotions have in your lives. If you do not express them and to offer you practical solutions to express them and let them go. So, they no longer have an effect on you and your overall wellbeing.

Negative emotions, such as, anger, sadness, fear (this is a huge area for many people), guilt, hurt, shame, conflict.

ANGER – Blocked love, high blood pressure, heart attack, strokes or heightened cholesterol.

SADNESS – Depression, low blood pressure, low energy levels, weakened immune system.

FEAR - Excessive Stress, PTSD, phobia and allergies.

GUILT – Lower healing energy.

SHAME – Skin problems.

CONFLICT – Cancer.

These are just some of the negative effects of harbouring a negative emotion that is not released or expressed in your body. Which leads us to the question of what is really holding you back in life?

WHAT IS HOLDING YOU BACK?

1. UN-EXPRESSED NEGATIVE EMOTIONS OF THE PAST

The truth is you and I do not link our challenges, illness and lack of motivation to un-expressed negative emotions in our bodies. This is what's holding most people back from being all they can be.

You see as children we learn very early on that emotions are not to be expressed and to feel emotions is wrong or we are wrong to feel them.

As young boy growing up whenever I cried, especially in public my parents would shout at me and tell me to be quiet and I was never allowed to express how I feel. Especially in my culture coming from Lagos, Nigeria, children where only seen, never heard. Growing up, I was constantly told that boys don't cry, only weak boys cry. Perhaps you have had similar experiences as me, but this is just a generalisation. I'm sure some people had a great upbringing and were loved and allowed to express their emotions and that is great but for most people in society that is not the case at all.

The goal here is to learn to express your emotions in every given moment and to create a space for your children if you have children to express themselves fully- And to validate their emotions so they are free from guilt, shame, embarrassment, fear, sadness and anger.

2. THE WAY YOU EXPRIENCE YOUR EMOTIONS

How you choose to experience your emotions would determine how you express them. There are two ways in which you could become aware of your experience:

BY ASSOCIATION

Association is living the experience. Viewing everything around you through your own eyes, meaning being a part of an event and experiencing it from the inside.

Try this out yourself, close your eyes and imagine floating up towards the ceiling. Now imagine looking down from your new vantage point. You do not see your body on the chair because you imagine you are in your body. Imagine floating down again, seeing the chair get closer and closer until you are back where you started. When you are inside your body, seeing pictures through your own eyes, then you are associated.

When you are associated, you feel the feelings (emotions) that go with the experience.

Phrases to identify when you are associated to an event, experience or situation:

In the experience, all there, in the thick of it, with it, caught up, in the flow, in touch

ADVANTAGES

Going through pleasant experiences and memories in all its full richness and glory. Practicing or learning new skills.

Paying attention and being yourself.

DISADVANTAGE

Caught up into the experience that you are now too deep into it to work with it.

BY DISSOCIATION

Dissociation means separating, detaching, distancing yourself from an event or situation. You watch a movie, as it were, in which you can see yourself as the hero.

Now imagine floating out of your body, seeing your body sitting in the chair. Imagine you can go 'astral travelling' through the room, seeing your body from different viewpoints. Now float back down again. Your body hasn't left the chair, yet it appears you have. When you see yourself as if from the outside then you are dissociated.

When you are dissociated, you have feelings (emotions) about the experience.

Phrases to identify when you are dissociated to an event, experience or situation:

Out of it, laid back, on the sidelines, not with it, not all there, not quite you, out of touch.

ADVANTAGES

Reviewing your experiences to discovering meaning and patterns out of them. Learning from past experiences, so you can act and behave differently in the future. Taking a step back from unpleasant situations.

DISADVANTAGE

Being too far away from the experience to work with it.

Most people in society associate to negative emotions and dissociate form positive emotions now this is the wrong way in my opinion to express your emotions – Now one can argue that sometimes it's necessary or beneficial to associate to negative emotions to let it go – I would personally agree that is true just for acknowledging it and letting it go.

Now as a rule, think of your pleasant memories in an associated way to get the most enjoyment from them and your uncomfortable memories in a dissociated way to avoid the bad feelings. This way you keep your vibrational energy high.

3. COMFORT ZONE

People settle for something good or they just simply settle for something rather than going after what they truly want in life – And the biggest and the deadliest negative emotion that is responsible for this is non-other than "FEAR." It wouldn't be right (since we are talking about how to manage emotions, so they don't manage you) not to expand on this one emotion that really has a grip hold of many people in society.

WHAT IS FEAR?

Fear according to the Oxford Compact English Dictionary is defined as, "1. An unpleasant emotion caused by the threat of danger; pain, or harm. 2. The likelihood of something unwelcome happening."

According to Amyn Dahya, my spiritual mentor, *"Fear is a powerful motivation, which causes us to act in a manner that often defies reason and good judgment. It is a force of repulsion that creates anxiety, pain, frustration and unhappiness."*

Fear is an illusion that resides only in the future. It uses the future as its weapon to destroy the present. And he goes on to say that, "Fear comes from our inability to embrace the unknown. It reigns in the absence of trust and causes us to be suspicious and paranoid. It is an illusion that resides in the mind, which makes it both powerful and weak."

F.E.A.R is an acronym that stands for, "False Evidence Appearing Real!" And it is only appearing real in the mind of the person that perceives the fear in the first place.

What Amyn Dahya meant by fear being both powerful and weak is simply that, "If you and I can create thoughts in our mind which gives this fear it powers then we can by the same token create thoughts that can eliminate this very fear in our minds. Take for instance if you put a glass of coke on the edge of a table and you saw that the table was unstable and, in any moment, now the glass will fall and break then in that very moment you can eliminate the fear of that glass breaking by moving the glass of coke to another table that is more stable. As soon as you do that you can no longer have the thought of the glass breaking anymore and instantly in that moment you have eliminated that fear from you mind. Try it out yourself; it works every time for me!

Fear can also be known as Phobias – A phobia is an extreme irrational fear or a dislike of a specified thing. A Phobia is when a person has an overwhelming response to an object or situation. A traumatic past experience that is difficult even to think about without feeling bad; whatever the cause the response is overwhelming anxiety. Phobias can vary enormously e.g. the fear of snakes, spiders, needles, heights, fear of flying, fear of open spaces etc.

BACKGROUND HISTORY

They are two main types of fears that we were born with and that is, "The fear of heights and fear of loud noises" All other forms of fear are abnormal and just an illusion created in our minds." The great news about this is we can eliminate phobias by using very simple NLP techniques.

As we can see we all have different types of fears that prevents or hold us back from giving, being, doing and having what it is that we want from life. I would like to mainly focus on some general fear within our societies such us:

- Fear of Rejection
- Fear of Being Judged
- Fear of Being Controlled
- Fear of Failure
- Fear of Helplessness
- Fear of Commitment
- Fear of Being Alone
- Fear of Not Being Enough
- Fear of Not Being Loved
- Fear of the Unknown
- Fear of Being Wrong
- Fear of Success

- Fear of Growing Old
- Fear of Public Speaking (The No.1 Fear in the world)
- Fear of Death (The Only Certainty in our lives)

These are very common fears and some or all these fears would have been your very own fear at a given point in time and may still be one of the fears you have readily present in your lives today. I personally know that I have experienced all these fears at various crossroads, in my own personal life.

You have two choices with F.E.A.R. – Fuck Everything And Run or Face Everything And Rise. Feel the fear and do it anyway and like all the other negative emotions in our lives we need to find an avenue for them where we can fully express and eliminate them. For us to, create a more compelling future.

Now that we know what is holding us back, it's time to free ourselves from it. It's time to break free from our negative emotions. It's time to let them go.

The rest of this chapter will provide you with two very powerful processes to help you manage your emotions.

The first one is for deep-rooted (through negative conditioning) negative emotions of the past like Anger, Sadness, Fear, Guilt and Hurt in that order. This process does require someone else to work with you. It cannot be done individually by yourself, someone has to guide you through the process for you to really get the benefits form it. This process is called, "HYET" (Healing Your Emotional Trail Process).

The second one is a simple easy to do meditation that you can do by yourself daily to eliminate stressful and unwanted negative emotions in any given moment. This is called, "Inner Cleansing Meditation"

Let's explore them individually now.

"HYET" (Healing Your Emotional Trail Process). It is a very powerful technique that I adapted from NLP and Timeline Therapy by Tad James. The process uses a few NLP tools combined but the fundamental technique is Timeline, which I refer to as Time-Trail in this book.

Before I take you through the step-by-step process I would like to introduce you to another simple but very powerful NLP tool called resource anchoring or positive emotions. You are going to need to establish a few resource anchors for your client to perform the HYET Process successfully.

RESOURCE ANCHORING/ POSITIVE EMOTIONS

Before we talk about what resource anchoring is, let us describe what an anchor is:

An Anchor is a stimulus, which is linked to and triggers a physiological state. Anchors are usually external. An Anchor is anything that accesses an emotional state and they are so obvious and widespread that we hardly notice them. Therefore, an anchor is an external stimulus, which is linked to a specific trigger e.g. a piece of music that reminds you of a very special someone while you were doing that special thing? Or a particular perfume that reminds you of your spouse, friend, mum or lover etc.

As human beings we are anchoring machines and we are doing

it every second of the day. A lot of the associations and links we make are very subtle and we are unaware of a lot of them.

Anchors are very important as we have positive ones and negatives ones and by identifying them we can through a simple technique collapse the negative ones and use the positive ones to assist us in eliminating our negative emotions or dramatically reducing their effects on our emotional state. Below I have outlined the main keys to anchoring and how you can actually create one.

There are five main keys to anchoring and they are:

1. The client must be in an intense state
2. The Anchor must be applied at the peak of the state
3. The stimulus used for the Anchor must be unique
4. The Anchor must be repeatable
5. The more time the Anchor is created the better the Anchor

These are the steps involved in creating an anchor:

1. Elicit an intense Associated State in the client
2. Provide a unique stimulus as the state reaches its peak intensity
3. Break the State with the client so their state changes
4. Test the Anchor by providing the same stimulus and notice they go into state

The real purpose of this section is to show you how resource anchoring is created.

If we can elicit a resource anchor from our client and anchor it – Then we can elicit a few more and anchor it in the same place as the first one. This process is known as, "Stacked Resource Anchoring"

Another name for resource anchoring is positive emotional states, such as, Love, Laughter, Confidence, Powerful, Certainty, Totally Energised just to mention a few.

Please read below to ascertain what states are preferred while anchoring.

The way this works is very simple pick any one of the states mentioned above below and follow the state elicitation script outlined below. Remembering to go into the state you are eliciting yourself, which gives your clients permission to do the same and enjoy the process, have fun doing it. As the client begins to go into the desired state we apply the anchor either on their knuckles or their shoulder by holding and pressing down your index finger. It is important that you apply the anchor the same way each time using the same finger each time. When you see the client coming out of the state you release the anchor. You will really need to have your sensory acuity switched on for this process; noticing everything about the client like, the way they move their entire body, the way they are breathing and using their facial expressions etc. If you feel the anchor is not strong enough then by all means, ask the client for another time when they were in that state. When done move to another state and for the purpose of HYET process you would need to stack about four to five states ensuring that the stack resource anchor is very strong and intense. The way you check this is very simple after you finish stacking the resource anchor then you do what we call a break state. There are numerous ways of breaking someone's state such as, getting them to stand up and turn around; if they are standing up you can break their state by asking them to move to a different position and shake their body; or you can pretend to smell something around them as though they have farted and then say, can you smell bacon or popcorn. You get the idea! Then test the anchor to see that they actually go into the states you've anchored, remembering to use the same finger on the same knuckle or the same shoulder. If there go into the states, then you've got yourself a great resource anchor if not it means you need to find more intense positive states and just ask your client for another time when they had those positive states in the past.

Preferred States For Anchoring

1. Naturally occurring states are most intense.
2. Vividly remembered associated specific memories in the past are less intense.
3. General memories of the past are even less intense.
4. Imagines or Constructed States are least preferred.

State Elicitation Script

1. Get into Rapport with your client.
2. Go into the Desired State yourself.
3. "Can you remember a time when you were totally   x'd?
4. "Can you remember a specific time?"
5. "As you go back to that time now... go right back to that time, float down into your body and see what you saw, hear what you heard, notice what you noticed and really feel the feelings of being totally
   x'd   ."

STATES FOR STACKED RESOURCE ANCHORING

- Powerful.
- Loved.

- Totally Energised.
- Confidence.
- Certainty
- Laughter.

Now that you have learnt how to establish a resource anchor you are ready. So here we go, let me take you through the process step-by-step.

HYET PROCESS – HEALING YOUR EMOTIONAL TRAIL

1 – BULD RAPPORT WITH YOUR CLIENT AND ESTABLISH WHAT NEGATIVE EMOTIONS THEY WANT TO RELEASE

Find out the emotion/s your client wants to release – **Anger/sadness/fear/guilt and hurt** and this is the order in which the emotions should be released. Ask: "Is it all right with your Unconscious Mind for you to release this **(name the negative emotion)** today and for you to be aware of it consciously?" Now you can release them individually or all together in one session. With HYET Process my usual preference is to help my clients eliminate all of the negative emotions (Anger, Sadness, Fear, Guilt and Hurt) in that order and any other emotions that is holding then back.

2 - ESTABLISH 4 OR 5 POSITIVE RESOURCE ANCHORS FOR YOUR CLIENT

Establish a resource anchor by following the instructions listed on page 5-8. This will be very useful for when the client starts to go into a negative emotional state during the process. E.g. when client has been asked to confront their negative experience and release it during the process or when the client abreacts whilst expressing how they felt about the event in the past.

Get the client to attribute a personal colour to each Positive Resources (PR). The colours become their personal 'Rainbow Colours', which is part of the healing process, hence the name, "Healing Your Emotional Trail Process" (HYET). For example:

Positive Resources (Emotions) Colours		Personal Rainbow
LOVE	=	RED
LAUGHTER	=	YELLOW
CONFIDENCE	=	BLUE
POWERFUL	=	GREEN
CERTAINTY	=	PURPLE

3 – ELICITING THE TIME-TRAIL

"We are going to play a game now called trust your unconscious mind. If you were to trust your unconscious mind and I asked you right now what is the direction of your past, where would you point to? Good, if I asked you right now what is the direction of your future, where would you point-to? Very good, and if I was to ask you where is now, where would you point to?

Now, ask the client, if you were to draw a line connecting the past to the present and the present to the future, can you now notice how that implies a line? That's your timeline."

4 – EXPERIENCING THE TIME-TRAIL

"Now, would you bring to mind your timeline?" Can you just float up above your timeline? Wonderful, now I want you to just float up even higher and higher now. Just keep floating so high now that the entire timeline seems only as long as a pen or pencil. And as you look at the timeline so far away, I want you to just float all the way back into the past. Go as far back as you want to in the past and stop anywhere you want to and tell me, how old are you? Okay, **(repeat whatever age they tell you)** now turn around and face now and float all the way back to now and tell me when you get there. Okay, now float all the way out into the future and keep going, go so far that you go all the way out into the future…way beyond now and tell me how old are you? Great, **(repeat whatever age they tell you)** you are doing just fine…now I want you to float all the way back to now and when you get back to now, just float directly above now and let me know when you get there.

"Come all the way back down to now, and float down into now and come back in the room." **(Pause)**

"How was that?" And I usually say at this point, "It's like having a mind trip without the drugs, this usually lightens the mood with a little chuckle from the client!"

5 – SHOW DIAGRAM OF TIME-TRAIL

Explain the importance of position A, B & C in relation to their timeline for example:

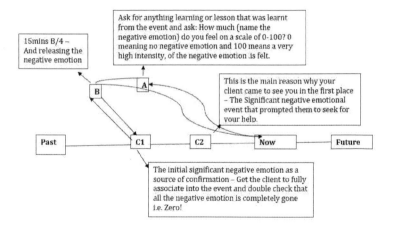

Position **A** is directly above the initially significant emotional event **C**

Position **B** is 15 minutes before and above the initially significant emotional event **C**

Position **C** is the actual initial significant emotional event.

6 - FINDIND THE ROOT CAUSE OF THE NEGATIVE EMOTION

Find out the first time your client ever experienced the first negative emotion (Anger) – Say, "I am about to ask you a really wired question and perhaps you may not know the answer consciously but if you were to know, when was the very first time that you felt **(name the negative emotion in this case Anger first then followed by next emotion when you finish healing Anger)** was it before, during or after your birth?"

BEFORE: "In the womb or before?"

WOMB: "What month?"

BEFORE: "Was it a past life or passed down through generations?"

    PAST LIFE: "How many lifetimes ago?"

    GENERATIONAL: "How many generations ago?"

AFTER: "If you were to know, what age were you?"

NOTES:

> ➤ If client says "I don't know the root cause or what the source is. "Respond with, "I know you don't know, but if you did...take whatever comes up...trust your unconscious mind."
> ➤ If the client says both genealogical and past life, work with the earlier one first, then the later one second.
> ➤ Ratify the change: Verify conscious acknowledgment of shift. When a major physiological shift occurs in the

client, be sure to mention it: " That was a big one, wasn't it?"

7 – BEGIN THE PROCESS ACQUIRE LESSON/S LEARNT AND DETERMIINE INTENTSITY OF THE EMOTION TO BE RELEASED

Begin the process by asking the client to float above their Time-Trail and float to the past (position A), which is directly above the ISEE of Anger (position C based on the root cause your client gave you above). Get the client to nod their heads to let you know there are there.

The next step is to now provide your clients with the PR (Positive Resources) in Step 2 to their younger self. This will allow them to now have these PR virtually as well as physically.

How is this done?

By using the imaginary balloon scenario (Imagine you have a red coloured balloon representing the positive resource of love, based on your original stack resource anchor established above in step 2). Explain to your client that this is a very special type of balloon and it has been made from very special material. It doesn't matter how much you blow into the balloon or how big it gets, it never pops. So, you can go ahead and blow all the essence and energy of love into the red balloon. Blow all the love into your red balloon. Think of all the past and present love you've received, given or felt and blow the essence of that into the red balloon. Now, imagine, all the love that you will now receive as result of doing this process, imagine all the love that you will receive in the future and the ones you will give and blow it into the red balloon. Make it a very big balloon indeed and when you are done. Take the tip of the balloon and hold it tightly…Float down to the younger you (from position A down to position C) and place the tip of the balloon in their mouth and allow them to suck all that essence and energy in like a vacuum. See the smile on their face, as they take in, all the love depicted or represented in the colour red. Once you are done then float back up to position A and nod your head when you get there to let me know you've arrived.

Now repeat the above process for the remaining PR anchors you have established in step 2. In this example you will now do the same for, Laughter with a yellow balloon; Confidence with a blue balloon; Powerful with a green balloon; and finally, Certainty with a purple balloon.

We allow our client to pass on their PR anchors to the younger version of themselves in the past. This is a very important process as these are the PR anchors that our client needed to be able to handle and deal with what had happened in the past. Explain to the client if they had, had access to these PR resources at the time of the event itself, then they would have dealt with it very differently.

On completion of the above process we now ask our client float down to position C and look at the younger version, of themselves glowing with energy and radiating love, laughter, confidence, powerful and certainty in all the various colours of their personal rainbow. Then we ask them hold hands and hug the younger version, of themselves, look intently into their eyes and say, "I LOVE YOU"…(and for most clients this will be the first time of expressing self-love). So give them a few moments here and have some tissues on standby. You usually get a few teary eyes here. I also occasionally, get them to say, "I LOVE YOU" using their various positive resources as in – Say, I love you with love in your voice; Say, I love you with laughter in your voice etc.

You only do this section once at the beginning of the process when you are working on releasing anger. (The first negative emotion to release)

When you move on to releasing, sadness, fear, guilt and hurt or any other negative emotions. You only remind your client that they already have all the emotional resources they need, to handle these negative emotions. Here, I just remind them of their PR and personal rainbow colors that each one represents.

ACQUIRE LESSONS - Ask your client to float above their Time-Trail and go back directly above the very first event to position **A**. Here ask: In order to release this emotion easily, it sometimes helps to have learned whatever you needed to have learned from the event. Now sometimes these lessons need to be conscious, and sometimes these lessons need to be unconscious. So out of curiosity, is there anything you need to learn consciously from this event, the learning of which will allow you to let go of this emotion easily and effortlessly?"

(If your client says "No") Say, "Great, then just allow whatever lessons there are for this event to remain unconscious."

(If your client says, "Yes") "What positive lessons are in this event? The learning of which will empower you and allow you to release the emotion from your past easily and move you to the future with healthier decisions and actions in your life." **(If**

necessary, reframe the lessons so they are positive, about the self, and focused on the future.)

DETERMINE THE INTENSITY OF THE EMOTION

Whilst still in position **A** are you aware of position **B** – Before the event, and position **C** – The actual event? Great, now on a scale from 0-100, 0 being no emotion what so ever, and 100 being the most intense **(name the negative emotion in this case anger)** you have ever felt, how much **(name the negative emotion in this case anger)** is in your body? **(If less than 50)** Super, then this one will be really easy to release. **(If more than 50)** Great, then you will really be able to feel a significant shift as you release this emotion."

Here I usually find that because of the balloon process above that the intensity of the first emotion (Anger) is usually sometimes very low like under 50 and that is okay – But not in all cases, just in most cases from my experience and feedback from my certified, "Empowerment Coaches."

8 - RELEASE THE NEGATIVE EMOTION

Whatever number your client gives you above in step 7 use it here. Let's say, your client told you that the intensity for their anger was 45 for example.

Now I want you to float above to position **B,** which is just opposite position A – 20 minutes or just before the event. Nod your head when you are in position B. Great, now I want you to begin to release this anger from 45 – 0 and only let me know by nodding your head when you are at 0. This way, I would know to continue with the process.

Allow your unconscious mind to support you in whatever way it needs to today – So the negative emotion can just release. Go ahead now and begin to release this anger now. Just let it go... **(Wait a moment; use sensory acuity to mind read that the negative emotion has gone.)** Now, ask where is the emotion?

(If they say it's still there) "Sorry, I didn't mean to rush you. Just go ahead and keep letting it go, and when you get to 0 from 45 just let me know by nodding your head." Allow your unconscious mind to support you in whatever way it needs to support you in releasing this **(name negative emotion in this case anger)** now. **(Wait for them to nod then play the role of devil's advocate (see below for details), as you want the client to truly convince you that the negative emotion is completely gone)**

(If they say it's all gone) "Great, now on a scale from 0-100, 0 being no anger what so ever, and 100 being the most **(name negative emotion in this case anger)** you've ever experienced, you're probably at a 10 or 20 then right?" **(If they say, "No, it's 0" then continue with the process)** Anything other than 0, we want to make sure we remain in position B until all the negative emotion is completely gone.

THIS NEXT SECTION IS NOT A SEPARATE STEP IN THE PROCESS – IT HAPPENS THROUGH OUT THE PROCESS:

SHAPING YOUR CLIENT

Shaping is when your client is following your instructions or when you spot them through sensory acuity that they are shifting during the process – You want to praise them and encourage them to do more of the same by saying, "you are doing a great job...well done I can see you really shifting, that's it, just let all that emotion go now, thank you for your honesty, thank your unconscious mind for allowing you to honour yourself in such a beautiful way today etc."

9 - PLAYING DEVIL'S ADVOCATE

(If your client says the negative emotion is completely gone, you say) "Really? No emotion what so ever? Well can you prove it? Can we test it to make sure it's completely gone? Just go ahead now and float right back down into position **C** – Seeing the event through your own eyes, and even though you can remember that you use to have that negative emotion notice how that negative emotion is no longer there. It's kind of like you are remembering this event differently now. So, on a scale from 0-100 how much **(name the negative emotion in this case anger)** is in your body? **(If 0)** Are you sure? How can that be? Are you positive? Really? Congratulation! Just go ahead and float up to position **B** – Before the event and continue with the process.

(If anything other than 0) "Great, thank you for your honesty, I appreciate you for that. Just go ahead and float back up to position **B**, and this time just keep going up higher and further back, go so high and far back that all of the emotion completely releases. And just nod your head as soon as it has completely and totally released." **(Go back and repeat step 8)**

10 – RETURNING TO NOW & THE HEALING PROCESS

Float above to position **B**, from there "Now, come back to now above your time-trail only as quickly, easily and effortlessly as you can let go of all the **(name the negative emotion in this case anger)** along your Time-Trail. And to ensure that the emotion has released from your past, I want you to stop at all the events along your Time-Trail that you have experienced **(name the negative emotion in this case anger)**. Just make sure the negative emotion is completely released. And do the same for all subsequent events in your past that you experienced this anger. Float all the way, back to now keeping your eyes closed and nod your head when you are back at now to let me know that you are back.

Test to make sure all the, **(name the negative emotion in this case anger)** is all gone. Ask the client to take a look at their past and check from now, right up to the ISEE (Initial Significant Emotional Event), for anger (the root cause of anger) or vice versa and make sure all the, **(name the negative emotion in this case anger)** is all completely gone.

If the client, say's anything other than completely gone then repeat steps 8 – 10.

If the client say's yes, it's completely gone then we move on to the Healing Process.

This is a very important part of the whole process, where the

HYET name was formed. Explain to the client that their **4 or 5 PR anchors** depicted or represented by their chosen colours now forms the basis of their very own rainbow colours – And like a rainbow all this colours are attached together and there is no way of telling where one begins and finishes. E.g. If the 4 PR anchors were **(Love, Laughter, Confidence and Certainty)** and they are depicted or represented by the various colours **(Love=Red, Laughter= Yellow, Confidence = Blue and Certainty = Green)** then this will form the basis of their personal rainbow colours. **Red, Yellow, Blue & Green.** Get the client to imagine a big paintbrush handle. This is no ordinary paintbrush because it has 4 or 5 brush sections underneath the handle (the number will depend on how many PR anchors you and your client have decided to go with. In this example it will have four separate brush sections **(Red, Yellow, Blue & Green)**. Get the client to imagine dipping their special paintbrush into their reservoir of their new PR anchors **(Love=Red, Laughter= Yellow, Confidence = Blue and Certainty = Green)**. Get them to take the paintbrush and go all the way back to the **ISEE** for the anger and tell them to **HEAL** the event by painting it with their personal rainbow colours. Get them to continue to heal all other subsequent events with similar emotions across their Time-Trail all the way back to now.

After the healing process, ask your client to look back at their time and ask them to tell you what they see (offer no suggestions here, just listen and take note of what they say). This will give you a good indicator as to how well the process as worked them. Remember to always be calibrating changes and minor shifts in your client throughout the process.

Well done! You have successfully, assisted your client to release and heal one of their negative emotions in their emotional trail. Now you need to repeat the whole process from **Step 6–10** for the remaining negative emotions, for example   sadness, fear, guilt, hurt etc.

Remember in step 7 you no longer need to repeat the balloon process just acquire the lesson/s and determine the intensity of the emotion and move on to step 8.

By releasing and healing, anger, sadness, fear, guilt, hurt and any other negative emotions your client maybe experiencing in the past; you will have succeeded in helping them healing their entire emotional trail.

11– TEST

Test the whole process by asking them to take a look at their past and double check and triple check that they are no issues in the past or their emotional trial that causes them anymore pain or discomfort –All the negative emotions have been completely and successfully released and healed. At this stage it's always a resounding YES! Just get them to describe what they see, they may say, "Colours". Ask them what colours? Once they have listed their colours. Ask them what those colours represent or depict for them personally. At this stage they really should know their PR anchors and what colours they represent off hand.

Now to complete the process we want to provide our client with their new PR anchors (which they now have in the past and in the present moment) in their future. We do this by getting our clients to imagine they are superhuman and possess the power to move like the speed of light (their very own version of the Flash). With this in mind we get them to hold their special paintbrush and dip it into their reservoir (colours) of PR anchors and on the count of 3 they paint their future from now to beyond this lifetime in just a few seconds. Tell your client to get ready for a ride of a lifetime 1, 2 and 3 go, go and go! Go way past this lifetime painting and healing your future and stop. Float all the way back to now in slow motion and look down and tell me what you see as you float back? Keep shaping your client throughout the process! Tell them to let you know by nodding their head when they are back at now.

12 – LIFE-REFRAME

Tell the client to look at the past, present and future and ask them to tell you what they see, hear and feel. Offer no suggestion and just take note of what they are saying and calibrate minor shifts in physiology. Here you say, "Everything that has happened to you in the past, up until now, happened for a reason. We can't change what happened, but we can change the meaning we've given to what happened. All emotions are supposed to be released and let go off in the moment but when we hang on to them they develop into something else in our physical body. Your life is absolutely perfect, and you have no problems and now that you have successfully released and healed your emotional trail – Does that mean you will not, feel anger or feel sadness or fearful or guilty or hurt in the future? No, not at all, you will feel all these emotions again in the future. The secret is to express them and release them in the moment –And you now have all the resources you need to do so with your PR anchors, which you never had before today. You now have the following PR anchors (mention the PR anchors and the colours they represent here). The real power of these virtual anchors is the more you use them the stronger they get. Get outfits in your various colours and wear them regularly making a conscious connection to them every time you wear your personal colours. Buy cups and mugs in your various colours and use them regularly. Create an A4 lamented large writing of the PR anchor in the colours of your personal rainbow and place it on your wall in your bedroom. Get creative on ways of using your personal rainbow colours daily. This will make them stronger over time.

13 – END OF COACHING SESSION

Conclude your session by saying, "Well done, now in a moment you are going to open your eyes and come back into the room…Only open your eyes and come back into the room as quickly, easily and effortlessly as you can accept all these suggestions for you. Making sure your time trail is arranged and organized in the best way that is most comfortable for you. Go ahead and open your eyes. Offer your client a glass of water…and tell them their body will be going through a significant shift as old neurons are breaking away and new neurons are connecting with each other. Some people may experience these feelings for a few days after the process.

There you have the, "Healing Your Emotional Trail Process" (HYET). This process cannot be done on yourself by yourself. You need someone to follow the instructions and work on you or you follow the instructions and work on someone else.

HYET TESTIMONIALS

Here are a few students of mine who have gone through our 7 Days Empowerment Coaching Certification Training and experienced the process first hand. This is what they had to say about the process:

"WHEN I HEALED MY EMOTIONAL TRAIL, TOSIN CAUSED ME TO SEARCH WITHIN MYSELF. I FOUND THAT I HAD ISSUES WITH MY FATHER, WHO I LOVE, THAT I COULD FINALLY RESOLVE. FOR YEARS I'D BEEN LOOKING FOR MY FATHER'S APPROVAL OF ME, YET AFTER WORKING WITH TOSIN I NOW REALIZED, THAT I HAD ALREADY SURPASSED HIS EXPECTATIONS, IN FACT, OUR DIFFERENCES ARE NOW RESOLVED. I NOW LOVE MY FATHER FOR LOVING ME. EMOTIONAL TRAIL HEALED! THIS IS THE DIFFERENCE THAT MAKES THE DIFFERENCE IN MY LIFE, THANKS MATE."

DALE ALLEN - AUTHOR OF THE BOOK ON CHEMICAL SAFETY – SEVRON

HEALING YOUR EMOTIONAL TRAIL WITH TOSIN, HAS ALLOWED ME TO NOT ONLY DEAL WITH ALL THE EMOTIONAL DISTRESS I WAS EXPERIENCING IN MY LIFE. FROM SADNESS, ANXIETY AND LOW CONFIDENCE TO RECEPTIVE SELF-

SABOTAGING BEHAVIOURS AND ANGER. I WAS ABLE TO ESTABLISH ROOT CAUSES FOR THE WAY I WAS BEHAVING AND DEALING WITH LIFE AND ENABLE ME TO BE MYSELF, WITHOUT MY PAST AND EMOTIONS HOLDING ME BACK. I WAS ABLE TO INVENT MYSELF AND REDUCE MY EMOTIONAL DISTRESS BY GETTING A GRIP ON MY MIND. NOTHING CAUSES MORE EMOTIONAL DISTRESS THAN THE THOUGHTS WE THINK.

HEALING YOUR EMOTIONAL TRAIL WITH TOSIN ALLOWED ME TO DO A BETTER JOB OF IDENTIFYING THE THOUGHTS THAT DIDN'T SERVE ME AND SUBSTITUTING THEM WITH MORE USEFUL THOUGHTS. I WAS ABLE TO LET GO OF THE PAST AND CREATE POSITIVE MEMORIES. I AM NOW ABLE TO DEAL WITH CIRCUMSTANCES IN A COMPLETELY DIFFERENT WAY AND UNDERSTAND WHO I AM AND THE ABILITY TO LOVE MYSELF. I FEEL FREE AND EMPOWERED. THANK YOU TOSIN

SHELINA MAWJI – FOUNDER PRESS PAUSE LTD.

I NEVER HAD ANY KNOWLEDGE ABOUT THE HEALING YOUR EMOTIONAL TRAIL PROCESS UNTIL I MET AND WORKED WITH TOSIN OGUNNUSI OF MPOWERMENT I KNEW THAT I WAS STRUGGLING WITH MANY ISSUES BEING A VICTIM OF DOMESTIC ABUSE, SUICIDAL TENDENCIES AND HAD STARTED UP A BUSINESS, WHICH WASN'T GROWING BECAUSE I HAD NO TRUE BELIEF, IN MYSELF, MY BUSINESS OR MY CAPABILITIES. I LEARNT SO MUCH DOING THIS PROCESS AS IT ENABLED ME TO REVISIT MY PAST AND RECOGNIZE THE EMOTIONS OF HURT THAT I WAS CARRYING WITH ME AND THE BAGGAGE I WAS CARRYING THAT WAS HOLDING ME BACK FROM LIVING MY LIFE TO MY FULLEST POTENTIAL. THE COMBINED, RESOURCES

OF NLP & HYET TEACHINGS PLUS THE ACTUAL PRACTICAL LEARNING TIME REALLY HELPED ME TO FULLY GRASP THE CONCEPTS AND TECHNIQUES OF IMPROVING NOT ONLY MY LIFE BUT ALSO THE LIFE OF OTHERS. I FELT CONFIDENT IN MY ABILITY TO START GROWING MY BUSINESS AND GETTING MORE CLIENTS. TOSIN IS AN EXCELLENT TRAINER. HE'S KNOWLEDGEABLE, PATIENT, ATTENTIVE AND EXPLAINED THINGS VERY WELL, MAKING IT EASY TO GRASP EVEN COMPLEX IDEAS. SINCE ATTENDING I HAVE ALREADY TAKEN ON CLIENTS AND EXPANDED MY BUSINESS AND ALSO IMPROVED AS A PARENT AND WIFE. THANK YOU TOSIN AND MPOWERMENT.

MICHELLE WATSON - AUTHOR | BOOK CREATION MENTOR & PUBLISHER | MULTI-AWARD WINNING SPEAKER | COACH

HAVE YOU EVER HAD A TIME IN YOUR LIFE WHEN YOU JUST CAN'T THINK OF A SOLUTION TO A PROBLEM AND YOU FEEL STUCK AND HELPLESS? IF YOU'VE BEEN THERE WITH ME IN SPRING 2017, YOU WOULD HAVE SEEN THE STARRY NIGHT SKY FROM THE WINDOW IN TOSIN'S HOUSE IN NORFOLK, ME SITTING IN FRONT OF MY UNPACKED MINI-SUITCASE, DUMBFOUNDED, AS MY PARTNER RANT AT ME ACROSS THE ROOM, "I AM NOT DOING THIS. I AM GOING HOME NOW!"

I'VE NEVER DOUBTED THE LOVE BETWEEN US BUT IT CAME TO A POINT WHERE WE GOT STUCK AT ENDLESS FINGER POINTING AND VICIOUS CYCLE OF REACTING TO ONE ANOTHER'S WORDS IN VIOLENT ANGER. THERE WAS NO COMMUNICATION AS WE CUT EACH OTHER SHORT AND ALL REASONS GO OUT OF THE WINDOW. THERE, IN A BEDROOM

THAT'S NOT MY OWN, I THINK TO MYSELF "IS THIS IT? I'VE INVESTED SO MUCH IN THIS RELATIONSHIP: ENERGY, FEELINGS, FINANCES, BUT I CAN'T MAKE HIM DO WHAT HE DOESN'T WANT TO DO. IS IT TIME TO CALL IT GAME OVER?"

YOU CAN GUESS HOW SURPRISED I AM WHEN AFTER ALL, MY PARTNER STAYED THE NIGHT AND EMERGED OUT OF THE SESSION WITH TOSIN, CALM AND SERENE. MY PARTNER HASN'T BEEN KEEN ON COMING AT ALL, BUT IT SEEMS THAT TOSIN HAD SUCCEEDED IN FORMING A RAPPORT WITH HIM.

I WENT THROUGH THE SAME PROCESS, CALLED HYET (HEALING YOUR EMOTIONAL TRAIL). IT INVOLVES BEING INTERVIEWED TO CLARIFY WHAT I REALLY WANT, REGRESSION HYPNOSIS TO GET RID OF PAST BAGGAGE AND NEW TOOLS TO DEAL WITH SITUATIONS AND CREATING A DAILY INCANTATION TO BE DONE FOR THE NEXT 90 DAYS AS PART OF THE PACKAGE.

NOW, I WOULDN'T SAY THAT IT IS ALL A MAGIC BULLET AS IT IS A LOT OF WORK AND CHANGING THE PATTERN OF BEHAVIOUR IS NOT EASY FOR BOTH MY PARTNER, AND MYSELF BUT WE BOTH DECIDED TO GO THROUGH WITH IT. I CANNOT CHANGE MY PARTNER BUT I DECIDED THAT I AM GOING THROUGH WITH THE WHOLE PACKAGE EVEN IF HE DROPS OUT. YES, THERE HAD BEEN TIMES WHEN WE RELAPSED IN ANGRY ROWS AND I MADE 'EMERGENCY' PHONE CALLS TO TOSIN, BUT I STUCK TO THE PROMISE I MADE FOR MYSELF AND KEPT AT IT UNTIL THE END OF 90 DAYS.

SO HOW DID IT END? MY PARTNER AND I GOT MARRIED 6 MONTHS LATER ON 16TH NOVEMBER 2017, SURROUNDED BY FAMILY AND FRIENDS. AFTER GOING THROUGH THE HYET

PROCESS WE APPLIED THE TECHNIQUES TO STOP ARGUMENTS TO ESCALATE AND ALWAYS RESOLVE IT BEFORE GOING TO BED. ONLY TIME WILL TELL IF WE HOLD UP TILL THE END, BUT IF THERE'S ONE MESSAGE IN THIS STORY IT WOULD BE: BE STRONG ENOUGH TO STAND ALONE, SMART ENOUGH TO KNOW WHEN YOU NEED HELP, AND BRAVE ENOUGH TO ASK FOR IT. WE'RE BOTH GLAD WE DID ALL THREE AND FOR THE LAST TWO, WENT TO THE RIGHT PERSON: TOSIN.

DR. VIVIAN WIJAYA – CEO/OWNER/FOUNDER AT MANGA BIG BANG

HYET is a very powerful process but does require some time to complete. 1 to 1 sessions could take anything from 2 – 5 hours to complete depending on the individual you are working with. Everyone is very different and respond and react to the process differently.

INNER CLEANSING MEDITATION

I wanted to add a second process for eliminating negative emotions here that you can perform by yourself. It's a very simple yet powerful technique that I learnt from my spiritual mentor Amyn Dahya via his book, "Towards Zero Conflict."

According to Amyn, another very useful way of letting go of the painful feelings and negative emotions is through a meditation called, "Inner Cleansing." The Inner Cleansing meditation is an excerpt from the above book, "Towards Zero Conflict" on page 293-294. I highly recommend you get yourself a copy of this book

MEDITATION OF INNER CLEANSING

This meditation can be practised at any time, as long as you are in a quiet, comfortable setting. Make sure you are sitting or lying in a position where you are 100 per cent comfortable. Relax yourself and breathe freely.

Now close your eyes and imagine:

You are in a small, dark room. It is very, very dark. See the darkness and feel it for a minute or so.

You are very uncomfortable in this dark room. You do not like it at all. Imagine this discomfort and feel it for a few moments.

Then, think about the issue that is causing you feelings of pain, anger, or frustration. Focus on this issue and feel the frustrations. Allow these feelings to leave your body and to fill up the dark room.

Now you are all alone in this small, dark room, surrounded by your feelings of anger, hurt, pain and frustration. Take a few moments to experience these feelings.

Now, imagine that your hands are groping against the walls of this dark room. Suddenly, you push against a window and it starts to open. Outside of this window, there is a beautiful, warm, peaceful and loving Light.

As the window opens, this Light begins to come towards you. But, it cannot enter the dark room as long as your feelings of frustration and pain are present.

So, you take a broom and start to sweep these feelings (negative emotions) out of the window. As each feeling (negative emotion) leaves, a beautiful, bright, warm ray of Light replaces it.

You keep sweeping these feelings (negative emotions) out. You tell them, "It's time to go. I have no room for you in me."

You keep sweeping them out and as they leave, you welcome the warm, beautiful Light that fills up the room.

Now, you have said goodbye to all your pain, anger and frustration. They are gone. The room is full of Light. Look at this Light. Feel it, experience it.

There is no more room for darkness in you. You only have room for Light, nothing but Light.

Keep looking at this beautiful Light and savour it for as long as you wish.

When you are ready you may open your eyes.

By using this meditation, with practice, you will feel calm, peaceful and light. Practise this meditation as frequently as you wish. In fact, each time you feel uptight and unhappy at the end of the day, take a few moments and perform Inner Cleansing. Remember, you must be in a calm, peaceful setting with no distractions to achieve the most from your meditation.

HYET is very powerful for dealing with deep-rooted negative emotional issues and negative conditioning whilst Inner Cleansing Meditation is very useful for daily stresses and negative emotions that you encounter after going through the HYET process. I see it as another way of maintaining an on-going approach to your emotional stability and emotional intelligence.

Emotional intelligence is being able to choose at any given moment to completely access your emotion or not access your emotion and the skill to experience your emotion at a given moment, at the same time, being able to describe it or to reflect upon it without experiencing the negative side effects.

SUMMARY EMOTIONS – WHAT IS HOLDING YOU BACK?

- What is an emotion? And emotion is a strong internal feeling derived from one's circumstances, mood or relationships with others
- The Key here is to learn how to manage your emotions not the other way round.
- You possess both positive and negative emotions within you e.g. Love, Joy, Peace, Happiness, Bliss, Excitement, Anger, Sadness, Fear, Guilt, Hurt and Shame.
- What is holding you back? For most people it's all the unexpressed negative emotions in their body, not knowing how to express them and settling for a comfort zone (Fear).
- The question is which fear is holding you back? Is it a Fear of Rejection, Being Judged, Being Controlled, Failure, Helplessness, Commitment, Being Alone, Not Being Enough, Not Being Loved, The Unknown, Being Wrong, Success, Growing Old, Public Speaking or Death?
- What does FEAR stand for, "False Evidence Appearing Real," here you have tow options open to

you. "Fuck Everything And Run" or "Face Everything And Rise"

- Feel the Fear and Do it Anyway
- How can you release and let go of your negative emotions? By Using, "HYET" (Healing Your Emotional Trail Process) for deep-rooted negative emotions and Inner Cleansing Meditation for daily stresses and unwanted feelings.
- Remember as a general rule in life - Associate to all the good and pleasant emotions and Dissociate from all the bad unpleasant emotions.
- Emotional Intelligence is being neutral to your daily experiences. When something bad happens stay calm and neutral and when something good happens stay calm and neutral. This is just the same coin, with two different sides and we can learn from both experiences.

Promise yourself to be so strong that nothing can disturb your peace of mind. Look at THE SUNNY SIDE OF EVERYTHING AND MAKE YOUR OPTIMISM COME TRUE. THINK ONLY OF THE BEST, WORK ONLY FOR THE BEST AND EXPECT ONLY THE BEST. FORGET THE MISTAKES OF THE PAST AND PRESS ON TO THE GREATER ACHIEVEMENTS OF THE FUTURE. GIVE SO MUCH TIME TO THE IMPROVEMENT OF YOURSELF THAT YOU HAVE NO TIME TO CRITICISE OTHERS. LIVE IN THE FAITH THAT THE WHOLE WORLD IS ON YOUR SIDE AS LONG AS YOU ARE TRUE TO THE BEST THAT IS IN YOU!

CHRISTIAN D LARSON

DIFFICULTIES IN YOUR LIFE DO NOT COME TO DESTROY YOU, BUT TO HELP YOUR REALISE YOUR HIDDEN POTENTIALS AND POWER. LET DIFFICULTIES KNOW THAT YOU TOO ARE DIFFICULT...

DR A.P.J. ABDUL KALAM

CHAPTER 5
PURPOSE – WHY ARE YOU HERE?

"The Origin is Light, Light brings Life, Life brings Experience, Experience brings Knowledge and Knowledge brings Light. Such is the Cycle of Life."

Inspired by Source and written by Amyn Dahya

What is your purpose? Who are you? Why were you born? What is your big why for living or existing? What are you passionate about? What excites you? What are you good at?

Have you ever caught yourself asking any of these questions above?

For most of you that are normal human being, whatever that means to you because quite frankly some of you are aliens from out of space (Just to clarify what I mean by aliens; some of you are just freaks of nature like Lionel Messi, Rory Mcllroy, Tiger Woods and Christian Rolando who just jump out of their mothers wombs and knew exactly what to do in life)...But for those humans amongst us you've asked these questions several times of yourself right?

I personally believe you have found your purpose when you

love what you do, you do it so well, the world needs it and they are willing to pay for it to get it from you. Now that is what I call your true "PURPOSE" in life.

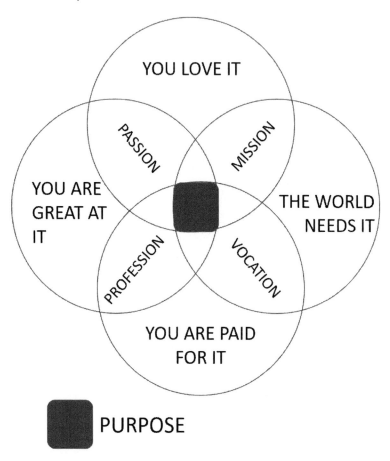

PURPOSE

I believe the world is like a giant jigsaw puzzle and you, me and everyone else is a piece of that jigsaw puzzle called planet earth. And each piece has a pivotal role in completing that whole picture – Meaning without you the world is not complete.

Imagine if you had a 1000-piece jigsaw puzzle and you misplaced just one tiny piece of it... Now I'm sure you would agree with me that no matter what you do that jigsaw puzzle will never be complete right? Unless you buy a new one and replace the missing piece...that's how important you are to the world. It's very important that you find out what you stand for and act upon it. Now some of you might be saying, "me? I'm not that important, little old me, what difference can I make in the world?"

If that's you then listen carefully to what the Dali Lama said, "If you feel you are too little and insignificant to make a difference in life then spend a night in a closed room with a mosquito and I promise you, you would soon realise how powerful and significant you are."

Your only job on this planet is to seek out what it is that you are passionate and in love with and learn how to do it well, make sure is something that would benefit others and people are willing to pay you for it to get it. When you know what that is then you have found your purpose meaning you have found your rightful place where your jigsaw puzzle piece fits.

Finding your Purpose in life is one of life's major celebrations.

As earlier explained, purpose in one's life is what is at the centre of your heart of hearts. It is the composite of your passion, mission, profession and vocation. Meaning you love it, the world needs it, you are great at it and you are paid for it. Even if you weren't paid to do it, you would do it anyway.

Now some people find this earlier on in life, some later on in life and the sad thing is, others never find it in this lifetime.

The question is do you know what your purpose is in life? And if you know are you fulfilling it?

HOW DO YOU FIND YOUR PURPOSE?

"We are all visitors to this time, this place. We are just passing through. Our purpose here is to Observe, to Learn, to Grow, to Love... and then we return home."

Australian Aboriginal Proverb

I love this proverb because for me it really sums it up in a nutshell. So if this is true and I belief it to be personally then it goes to show that what you decide to do for a living in the world is almost irrelevant as long as you are observing, learning, growing and loving.

I have often in the past caught myself saying, am I on the right path and am I doing what I'm supposed to be doing? If I am then why am I not flourishing in it, why is it so difficult to get clients to work with? I'm good at what I do, and I do it well and in some cases better than does that appear to be doing better than me in the same area? So, what am I doing wrong here?

Have you ever asked these questions of yourself? Notice, that there is a lot of, "WHY?" questions. I was asking myself all the wrong questions, so if you are doing that to yourself please stop it now.

A few months ago, I was watching a video online and it was Opera, interviewing a lovely lady (her name escapes me at the moment) on the topic of purpose and she asked the question that we are all dying to know, "How does one know if there are on the right path and on purpose?"

Her answer was equally as brilliant as the question itself, she said, "You know you are on right path and on purpose if, you're not put in a position to betray yourself." Wow, what a revelation indeed.

She then went onto say that everyone is on the right path, but the challenge is they are not managing it well. What does that mean? It means they have taken a detour – And a detour to me, means that you are forcing things to happen rather than allow them to unfold, either through desperation and fear of wanting to make ends meet.

You are betraying yourself by not honouring yourself and not following through on your actions (what you say, you are going to do). As in you've taken your eyes off the cause or mission of why you started on this path in the first place. Now this all made sense to me and I realised that I was always on the right path, I just wasn't managing it well because I took my eyes off the ball on a few occasions.

So, here's the thing you need to know and remember, "You're on the right path and you always have been from birth!" The second you were born you were endowed with the seed of greatness. You were empowered with a gift (a cause, a mission or a why) that only you came here to fulfil.

My belief is your purpose here on earth is to discover what that gift is and to fully express it for self and others – Through Observation, Learning, Growing and Loving everyone and everything on this planet because we are all connected.

Now as I said earlier some of the aliens amongst us find this gift very early in life and others later on in life and sadly some never find in this lifetime. So, if you are one of those people still struggling to find what your purpose is. Then let me offer some suggestions that I read and observed from other experts in this area that could perhaps help you to discover what your gift is. What I say gift, it means expressing your essence of who you are and how you express it is almost not really important as long as you express it. Meaning what job or work you do could almost be irrelevant here as long as you're observing, learning, growing and loving.

FIVE POWERFUL QUESTIONS TO FIND OUT YOUR PURPOSE

1. Who are you?
2. What do you do?
3. Who do you do it for?
4. What do they want or need?
5. How do they change because of what you do?

Take some time to contemplate these questions and answer each one as honestly as you can. To assist you further let me offer some suggestions with regards to each question.

WHO ARE YOU?

Here you want to look at your story so far, from as far back as you can remember, what was your life like? What did you do? Is there a common trend to your story? As in was there something that your repeated wanted to do growing up as a child? And are you doing it?

WHAT DO YOU DO?

Look at your career path here, as in all the jobs you've engaged in. Is it what you love to do? Perhaps you don't love it but you are extremely good at it? Are you happy with it? Does it pay you well? Would you do it for free if you had to? Is it something you would get out bed early for and stay late for?

WHO DO YOU DO IT FOR?

Do you love the industry you are in? Do you love the people within the industry that you interact with daily? What demographics are there? What is their gender, or do you work with both? What age groups do you work with specifically or do you work with all age groups.

WHAT DO THEY WANT OR NEED?

Here is all about the type of services and or products you provide for them and why? What is their main challenge, problem, frustration, obstacle, hurdle or barrier that they want to overcome? And finally...

HOW DO THEY CHANGE AS A RESULT OF WHAT YOU DO?

Outline here what the main benefit of your services and or product for the people you serve. How do they change? What is the transformation that takes place?

These questions, above, were inspired by Adam Leipzig in his TEDex talk about, "How to Know Your Purpose in 5 mins."

Another expert that I really like a lot and follow is Simon Sinek. He's famous for his book titled, "Know Your Why?" In the book he explains that finding your purpose starts with "WHY?" Why do you do what you do? And if you want to start out in something then ask why do you want to do it? Every successful company or individual today knows exactly what their, "WHY" is for doing what they do. It all begins with a mission, or a cause, in other words a reason for doing what they do.

Mother Theresa had a great cause, Nelson Mandela had a great cause, Mahatma Ghandi had a great cause, Tiger woods has a great cause, Tony Robbins has a great cause, Apple has a great cause, Amazon has a great cause, Google has a great cause, Hallmark Care Homes has a great cause. The question is what is your cause? What are you willing to put your life on the line for?

When you find your why? Then how and what you do becomes relevant. According to Simon Sinek when you find your why then people who share your beliefs and values will rally to your cause. People don't buy what you do they buy why you do it and he went on to say that, "The goal is to do business with people who belief what your belief and to hire people who belief what you belief because they will work for you with blood, sweat and tears not just for a pay check at the end of the month. I totally agree with Simon here.

QUESTIONS, FOR FINDING YOUR WHY?

1. What drives you?
2. What motivates you?
3. What inspires you?

The main cause for Simon Sinek can be summed up in this statement below:

"I Love My Job Is the Standard not the Exception!"

The question is can you honestly say, that you love your job? If you can then good for you, then you've found your calling.

If you are still struggling to find out what your passion is then my advice is to do something valuable to the world.

Doing something valuable in life gives you a sense of achievement and gives your life meaning. So, get good at doing what makes the world a better place to live in for all.

Someone once told me that doing what's valuable equals passion and success.

Sometimes you don't know what your passion really is, so doing something valuable for your world could turn out to be a passion and a success in the future.

How do you learn to do something valuable? By following these steps below:

1. EXPLORE – Learn about the world you live in and ask yourself what is the most pressing problems in the world today and how can I help, support or assist in solving these pressing problems?
2. SKILLS – Get very good at flexible skills that are transferrable into various industry sectors.
3. SOCIAL PROBLEMS – Research it and come up with creative solutions for them. To help bring balance and equality to the world.

Doing what's valuable means you are spending your working hours on this planet wisely and for the good of the whole.

This next section really sums up beautifully why we are here and what how purpose in life really is:

Amyn Dahya, who is my spiritual mentor and the author of, "Exploring Limitless Horizons – Understanding the Purpose of Life."

Through a conversation between the Origin (the creator) and an unborn soul, Maya, describes in detail the most frequently asked question in the world today, "Why are we here" What is the purpose of our existence?"

Before birth, Maya is an elevated soul who is at the stage where she says, "BE" and "IT IS!" Yet, in order to complete her spiritual journey, she must learn to gain Ultimate Freedom. In order to achieve this Freedom, she has chosen to be born on earth, where she is to be encaged in a human body that is limited by a mind that perceives everything through illusionary boundaries, called Horizons. Her world is to be comprised of Ten Horizons, which represent the limits that she must learn to transcend, if she is to gain Ultimate Freedom.

In Amyn's audio program, "Exploring Limitless Horizons" shows us practical methods by which we can identify, understand and transcend these Ten Horizons, through which we can achieve success, abundance and freedom in all aspects of our daily lives.

You see you are just like Maya and you too had a conversation with your Origin (the creator) before you were born on earth and encaged in your physical body that is limited by your mind that perceives everything through illusionary boundaries, called Horizons.

Let's explore what these Ten Limitless Horizons are and please bear in mind this information has been extracted from Amyn Dahya's audio program. It's so profound and powerful that it would be crazy to adapt it in anyway. I'm just merely passing on the information with Amyn Dahya's permission and blessings:

This insight will further expand your awareness and begin to re-awaken you to the precious gift of "EMPOWERMENT" that resides within you. This information (revelation) will surely open your eyes to new possibilities and really challenge what you have previously believed.

THE TEN LIMITLESS HORIZONS

"Life bring Light, Light brings Experience, Experience, brings Knowledge and Knowledge is Light! That is the full cycle of our Life"

This is the journey of the soul. To illustrate this dedication above, Amyn explains the conversation that Maya, a beautiful soul had with her Origin (Origin has many names, God, Source, Creator, Nature or whatever name you associate with it) just before she was born.

Maya was having this conversation with the Origin, where the Origin says to Maya, "You are now ready to take birth on this place called earth where you will be able to gain much knowledge and complete the journey of the cycle of your soul. Suffice to say that, Maya has been through the journey of her soul, gaining knowledge through every stage and every form of existence in life.

There are 7 worlds, this world (earth) is not the only world that we know, and the soul takes birth in these different worlds.

This world (earth), as we know it, has three dimensions, length, width and height. We see it as we see it, we perceive, and we feel our emotions, our thoughts and our reality is made up of that which our mind perceives but there are six others, where you do not necessarily take a form.

So, Maya had been through the six worlds and she had learnt a great deal but to complete her cycle (because the last stage of the cycle is gaining ultimate freedom), as long as she was on her journey, she started as a soul from the Origin. She started off as a ray of light that leaves the sun and through her journey, when you look at the ray and you look at the sun. The source and the ray, there is no difference because light is light and yet the ray is on its journey back into its source. When does it complete it journey, when it gains ultimate freedom that is the point of completion.

She is about to be born and the Origin says, "For you to gain ultimate freedom, because you have learnt everything that you need to learn as a soul. You are in such a state today, that when you say, "BE", "IT IS." You have got that power within you, but to gain ultimate freedom, I'm going to place you on the earth, where you will lose all your freedom.

I will encage you in a body. You're starting now as a soul with 99 senses and I'm going to put you in a body with only 5 senses. I'm going to take away all your freedom. I'm going to put within your body a mind, which will become another factor that will take away your freedom. In this world, I have placed Horizons everywhere, which are limits, which curtail your freedom. And the Origin, says, within this world of Horizons, within this world of no freedom, you can discover ultimate freedom. This world is the best place for you to complete your freedom"

The Origin asked Maya that up to now in the six worlds that you have been through, you have learnt about my light. You have learnt about me and tell me what you have learnt?

THE ORIGIN IS THE SOURCE OF ALL THINGS

So, Maya says, "The first law of your light is that you are the source. You are the Origin. Everything emanates from you. Everything begins with you and everything ends with you."

And the Origin, says, "Yes and this is the one truth that will be your key in the world that you are about to be born in. That since I am your source and that you have come from me. I will be with you at every step of this journey. This is a very important key during this lifetime that you are going to be given on earth. To gain ultimate freedom, is the knowledge of the fact that I am with you always."

Then he asks Maya, "What is the second law of my light?

THE ORIGIN IS PERFECTION ITSELF

And Maya says, "The second law of your light is you are perfection. Your light is completely perfect. It has no flaws. You are pure. You are perfect."

And the Origin, says, "Yes, and you in this soul stage are perfect too but when I send you in this world, I'm sending you in a state of complete imperfection. Nothing around you is perfect and within that imperfection, you will discover perfection.

Then he says, to Maya, "What is my third attribute?

THE ORIGIN IS UNIFORMITY

And Maya says. "Your third attribute is that you represent uniformity. Your light is uniform. It permeates through everything. There is noting that can block your light. It can permeate through universes because you are uniform."

And the Origin, says, "And I'm going to send you in a world that is completely un-uniformed. It is driven by change. Everything in this world is change. It is the complete opposite of uniform. And in the mist of this change, you will discover uniformity."

And he says, "What is the next attribute, what is the next law of my light?"

THE ORIGIN IS PURE CLARITY

And Maya says, "Clarity, your light is pure clarity. It is not like the light of the sun. It is not like the light of any form that we know. For example, electric light has heat associated with it and it is not clear, it does not have total clarity. Yet your light is completely clear."

And the Origin, says, "And the world I'm sending you into is completely obscure there is no clarity in this world but only in the mist of obscurity will you find clarity."

And finally, the Origin, says, "The fifth law of my light, what is it?"

THE ORIGIN IS UNITY (ONENESS)

And Maya says, "The fifth law is the law of unity that you are oneness, that everything about you is completely united. Everything is one and the Origin says and yet you are going to be born in a world where there is no unity at all. In fact, one of the fundamental laws of science of the world that you are going to be born in is on of fission; where everything starts from one and divides into two, into four, into sixteen and even into thirty-two. Everything from atoms to human begins to everything in this world is always ever increasing in dimension through fission; rather than having the unity of fusion but only in the mist of this lack of unity will you find unity."

So he says to Maya, "That the best place for you to complete your journey and to find ultimate freedom is in this world, where I have set these horizons."

And the Origin, says, "I have set ten horizons in this world and at the end of these horizons lies me. So, if you can transcend these horizons, you will discover me and you will discover ultimate freedom."

So, Maya is getting ready to take birth and she wants to know about these horizons, what are they?

And the Origin, says, "That a horizon is basically a limit. If we look on this earth and if we are standing before a sea we find a point where the sky meets the water and that is a horizon because in this world of 3 dimensions our eyes are limited to that horizon. If we travel towards that horizon then we reach another horizon because if you travel towards where the earth meets the water, you never get there. There's another horizon and when you travel towards it there's another horizon. So, yet, whilst there are limits there are illusions of limits. There are not real limits there are illusions because that which is real you can travel to and grab, but these horizons are illusions. So, while we live in this world of horizons, which tells us we are limited, we've been limited by illusions. So, in fact when we think of these illusions it reminds me of a situation when I was in Vietnam. There was a boy, a Vietnamese boy who had won the international Physics Competition worldwide and he was number one. He'd beaten kids from everywhere, so our company was involved in water treatment there, so we decided to give him an award of excellence. So, when we presented this award to him. I asked him (Amyn Dahya), "So how do you feel about this achievement?"

And he said, "This is the maximum achievement I'm ever going to get to. I have made it."

And Amyn, said, " Well, I congratulate you on your maximum achievement and let me tell you a story about a teacher and a student like you."

And Amyn, said, "The teacher and the student were looking at the stars and they said, let us aim for the stars, far out there in the sky's and let's get there. That would be our achievement. And so, they travelled the student and the teacher, and they land on that distant star. And they feel they have achieved the ultimate. Until the teacher says, to the student, look up again. There is another star and it's very far away. So, this is not the ultimate achievement maybe the ultimate achievement is the second star. And there travelled to the second star and when they look up, and there's yet another star. So, there is no ultimate achievement.

Success in life is not a destination it is a journey and so, when you look at horizons there are similar.

When the great Buddha, was of a young age. He decided he was going to go around the world in pursuit of enlightenment. So, what did he do?

He left the kingdom of his father, whatever clothes he was

wearing, that's all he took, and he decided to wonder through the forest, through the trees, through barren lands. And there were a few who followed him because they thought if he finds enlightenment then so will we. And Buddha travelled and travelled and travelled for years and didn't find enlightenment. And he could feel his body aging, but he could not find the enlightenment he was seeking. And then one day he goes to a river to clean himself and he looks in the water he sees his own image. And it makes him think, he looks at that image, he sees himself, but that's it. What lies beyond that image?

He could not find anything that lies beyond that image, that image was a limit but what he was trying to discover was the limitless. What lie beyond the limits and the coin dropped and he said, "My goodness, this is not the place to find enlightenment, the place to find enlightenment is in the mist of all these limits. In the mist of the world that I left that is the place to find enlightenment because if I'm amongst limits I will discover the limitless."

And he decides to go back. He gives up his life as a Hemet and decides to go back into the world, which he had left to seek enlightenment. Right in the mist of all the horizons that has been placed and that's where he found enlightenment.

So, the same is the situation with Maya, she is a very elevated soul. She knows all about the laws of the light. She's at a stage where she says, "BE" and "IT IS" and yet to gain that ultimate freedom, she is now taking up that physical form.

TIME – HORIZON NUMBER ONE

The first horizon is the horizon of time. The Origin says, to

Maya, "I've placed you in a world govern by time. Everything is limited by time. You will have a finite period of time to achieve this ultimate freedom. When you think of time. Time is a very limiting factor we are all govern by time. When we think of when we were young, when we think of when our children were young? When Amyn, thinks of his children who are now grown up and leaving home for university, he asks himself, "Where did the time go, it was just yesterday, how did they pass by him so fast? And yet that was a major horizon in his life that he failed to learn or to transcend. Time flies by us and what is the best way to transcend the horizon of time itself?

It is to achieve a state of timelessness because if you transcend time you get to timelessness.

What lies within timelessness?

The Origin lies within timelessness because the Origin has no beginning and no end. He is continuous. He is eternal so if we transcend the horizon of time we achieve timelessness.

How do we approach the horizon of time?

It is by living every second to its fullest, to stretch every second to its maximum.

When you think about your daily lives, you go to work, in the morning, and the whole day you spend trying to earn your daily bread; comes an end to the day. So many hours are gone. How did we stretch them? How did we maximize them?

It is by living in the present because the past is history, the future is to come but there is a very fine line that divides the past from the future, which is the present.

If we live completely in the present without been consumed by the worries of tomorrow or the memories of the past (many of us live in the past, many of us spend our day to day worrying about tomorrow), and those, seconds, which could have been stretched in the present are lost.

So, living in the present is of ultimate importance.

Amyn, shares an example that took place in Portugal. He travels around to different places to help people with healing and when he was in Portugal. It was a Sunday and they had three hours after which they had to stop the healing and Amyn had to rush to the airport and catch his flight to Malaga, Spain.

That morning they had a full appointment booked lots of people and while others found out his was town they just showed up at the hotel with no appointment booked hoping that maybe they will get a chance to be seen by him.

From 8am in the morning, there were all these people in wheel chairs and people who were ill just showed up at 8 am.

So, the organizer's said, there is no way you can see all these people today and make it to the airport in time. Amyn said, "Let's see how it goes, let them stay, we will do them all." And time went by and his three hours was complete, and they were all done. Those who had, appointments and those who didn't have, appointments and one of the organizer's said to Amyn, " How did this happen, each person came to you, you gave them all the time in the world. You listened to everything they had to say, you didn't rush anybody and in three hours they are all done. How did this happen? I was there and I still don't believe it has happened"

So Amyn asked him, "How many minutes in an hour?"

And he said, "Sixty"

And Amyn, said, "And that's where you are wrong, because you can make each minute very long. If you learn the key to gaining the maximum of the present there is a power that lies in the present that causes you to be able to stretch that present in an incredible way. It defies the laws of the clock."

So if we gain maximum living in the present. If we stretch each second to its maximum we are moving towards transcending the horizon of time itself, which makes us timeless beyond which we discover the Origin. So, by doing that we are bringing in or discovery the infinite within the finite.

MIND - THE SECOND HORIZON

The second horizon to transcend is the horizon of the mind because as the Origin says to Maya, "You are being caged in this body with 5 senses and I'm going to put a mind, which is going to tell you the opposite of what you are. What you are is a state of pure potential power, when you say, "BE" "IT IS" and your mind is going to tell you cannot be. So, while you who has the ultimate powers are going to be in this body, you're going to be limited by a mind that will keep telling you cannot be, cannot be, cannot be – And within that if you transcend the horizon of the mind then where do you end up?

You end up recognizing your true potential, which you are

right now, which is, "BE AND IT IS!"

How does one transcend the limitation, the horizon of the mind?

There are two keys is to remember the first law of the light of the source that the light of the Origin is the source. And that each one of us is connected to our source and that was the promise that the Origin gave to Maya; "I will be with you always in this world of horizons."

So, if we were to exercise the first key, to take a few moments each day and meditate on our source and reinforce that connection. That connection exists with all of us, but the mind does not recognize that connection. But when we meditate we transcend and we go in the direction of the light through the connection we possess. And through that our minds begins to perceive. A lot of times we are guided, all the times actually through that connection.

How often have you found yourself, you are about to enter into a situation and that little voice in you says don't do it? When you say, "Yeah, I'm going to make a lot of money, this is a great deal!" That something says, "don't do it!" And then you do it, you silence it because it's telling you what you don't want to hear, and you go into it and it blows up in your face. Sometimes, there are relationships and a man and a woman, they are going to get together and get married but that little voice is telling the girl don't do it, this is not where you should end up. This is not where your golden ring belongs, and she says but I've gone so far, now I'm obliged, I have to go through with it, the wedding invitations are gone, this is going to be a major disaster. I have to do it. Inside that root that connection is saying, "that is not your other half, but she silences it. She goes through with it only to find out it was not right.

So, when we think of the mind and when we think of the connection to our higher self; the practice of meditation is a fantastic key to really drawing inspirations to yourselves every moment of your life. You will make correct decisions. You will recognize the presence of the divine in every second of your life. Meditation is an essential part of it.

Not everybody understands meditation. People say, "I'm too old, now I'm fifty years old, when am I going to start? You know I'll probably have five more years to live and I'll be gone but meditation is such a thing that when you make that connection it takes a second.

You could have been trying, all your life and not realise that true potential or you could sit there for the first time and focus correctly and make that connection. It's never too late, so use that key to overcome the horizon of the mind, which is the biggest horizon to transcend.

The second key is the way we approach life, our attitude. Our attitude that our mind possesses, if our attitude is one of "BE" then "IT IS;" If our attitude is one of "CANNOT BE" then "IT IS NOT GOING TO BE."

Give you an example of a tropical rain forest. In this rain forest there were lots of trees, tall luscious green, rich trees and they had rain fall every afternoon. Millions and millions of drops of rain falling down then these trees are growing happily and at the bottom of these trees were smaller trees. Then one day there is a drought, there is no rain, there's no more water.

So, this big tall luscious tree starts to panic, they say, "We are not going to survive because the rain has stopped, there is no more water. We cannot live, we are going to die." And sure enough, they died because they have decided they cannot live in the absence of all this abundant of rainfall. We are going to perish, so they perished.

Think about it in terms of our lives today. Think about wealth and those rain drops, we have abundance and it's great and suddenly we don't have it any more and we think the world is over, we are finished. That's what happened to the trees, they perished but at the bottom there were some trees that said, "We will not perish, we will always be." They developed deep roots went deep into the ground and found every droplet that was deep down, and they drew those droplets. When the forest was dying these little ones came subject to attack by animals. Animals who were feeding on leaves had now decided to eat these guys because they were the only ones who were green. So, they developed thorns. I'm talking about the, "CACTUS!"

The Cactus is a very special plant because even when you go in a desert landscape, where there is nothing, it's a symbol of life. The Cactus said, "I WILL BE" and it developed its thorns to protect itself, dug its root deep down to find each droplet of water and it survived.

Whereas, all those tall trees that were majestic, look like the kings of the jungle perished. This Cactus on the other hand lived forever. So, we have think like the Cactus. If we run into difficulty, let's talk about the rainfalls as being equivalent to say, financial resources. We run into difficulty, we panic, we say, "Oh my God, the world is crumbling, or we are not going to make it" and everything we've built crumbles and collapses but if we say, "I am going to make it, I am going to be like that Cactus and I am going to find those little droplets wherever I can, but I am going to make it. Can you imagine against what odds those Cactus trees survive?

Try walking in the desert one day and realize that in the harshest of environments those little ones survived and so we have to be like the Cactus. And when we run into difficulties let us not lament and say, "it's over" let's say, "We possess the power of, "BE AND IT IS GOING TO BE" and we make it. And where are our thorns?

Around us and in our lives, we are always surrounded by those animals that came to eat those few green trees that were left but these are not animals that physically come to eat us, these are circumstances, they are people they bombard us with negativity. They are people that tell us we are never going to make it. They are people that tell us cannot be – And we have to develop thorns against them, we have to develop a thick skin. Whenever we listen to them, what they say bounces off our skin like water off a duck back.

Amyn had a friend who ones told him, "You can never accomplish this, cannot, cannot, cannot and each time Amyn proved him wrong. Every single time he proved him wrong and when they met recently, Amyn said to him, "Have you still not learnt?"

Develop those thorns, develop those thick skins, and do not let that negativity penetrate you. That is how we can be like the Cactus.

So, the horizon of the mind is really a very big horizon and before we move onto the next horizon. Amyn would like to share an experience he had in India.

There was a little boy about 20 years ago. This little boy comes to Amyn and say, "I cannot beg from you but let me clean your shoes and you pay me."

Amyn looked at him (a sweet little boy) and he said, "I'll tell you what, okay, go ahead and clean my shoes." So, as he's cleaning the shoes Amyn asked him, "So where are you from?"

He said, "He lived in this area"

Amyn said, "Who's in your family (because he thought the young kid should be in school)?"

He said, "I have five siblings, and my mother goes to work, three of my brothers and sisters go to school but I go out to work every day and I clean shoes. At least three of us are at school."

He keeps cleaning and Amyn asked him, "So what do you want to do with your life, where do you want to end up?"

The little boy, stopped cleaning Amyn's shoe, looked up and directly into Amyn's eyes and said, "I WILL BE A GREAT MAN!"

And Amyn looked at him and believed him.

What he said was completely contrary to the circumstance that he was in. Here was a kid cleaning Amyn's shoes for 1 Rupee, how can he become a great man?

And when he said, "A Great Man," he meant, I Will Be A

Great Man!

Everybody in the world would have said, "This guy will not make it, He will keep cleaning shoes until he grows older and maybe go and work in a factory and maybe learn his ABC and D but he's destined to be ordinary. And when Amyn, looked into his eyes, the way he said it, was, "BE AND IT IS" "I WILL BE A GREAT MAN!" And while we don't know what happened to him – Amyn is convinced that out in India somewhere is a great man who once cleaned his shoes – And his willing to bet on that. That was the power of the little boy's spirit.

When we look at what the Origin is saying to Maya about the mind, the limitation of the mind, gaining freedom. I think we have to also take into perspective what we see. For example, we see people in a famine in Ethiopia dying of hunger and we say, "My God, it must be their Karma, they must have done something wrong that is why they are been punished or it's so harsh but remember those souls are souls like Maya who have come into this world to discover ultimate freedom. And they have chosen this path of severe circumstances, within which they will transcend and break out and discover ultimate freedom.

So, when we look at these people around us who are less fortunate or appear to be less fortunate to us they may be very elevated souls who only have that one more step to take to complete their journey, while the rest of us are still plodding away. So, we cannot draw conclusions when we see people like that. They are people who are born in extreme wealth but under such difficult circumstances and we look at them and say, "Gosh, I feel sorry for them" but they have chosen their destiny, they have chosen this part of their life in this world to gain ultimate freedom, to complete the lessons and perhaps those people in Ethiopia who were dying of hunger had chosen to gain ultimate freedom from the most strongest of pain one can imagine and when they transcend it. They have completed their journey.

We cannot generalize, we cannot look at people and say, "This is punishment, this is good, and this is bad because each soul comes to transcend these ten horizons. Depending on which horizon one has to transcend one picks those circumstances.

RESOURCES - HORIZON NUMBER THREE

The Origin says to Maya that the third horizon is resources. What are resources?

Resources can be wealth. Can be intellect. Can be capabilities. Can be skills. All these things are tools, there are resources but there are horizons because if we don't have them we believe we cannot achieve but there are illusions of horizons. So, when you transcend the horizon of resources. When you go beyond the limitation of resources, where do you end up?

You end up in abundance, which is the Origin. The sum of everything but how do you transcend the horizon of resources?

We are always pressed by those limitations. In "Parables from the Origin" one of Amyn Dahya's inspired books, he shared a story of two little kids a boy by the name of Ibrahim and a girl by the name of Sarah. This is before humanity became what it had become, they are running around in the forest and during the daytime they are learning lessons about nature and the forest. The laws of the forest and during the evening, during the night they are learning lessons about the spiritual. So they are running around and one day they come to a place where there are seven tall trees. These trees have their roots that go into the core of the earth and they are as tall, as tall can be. They are touching the sky and they are seven trees and in the middle of the seven trees is a fountain. Like a fountain of water, it's coming out and flowing like a mushroom. So, they stop, and the first thing Sarah does is jump in to get a drink of some water because she is thirty and the forest has always provided for her. She tries to take a drink of water and finds it is not water. So, she is upset and said, "This fountain has lied to me, it looks like clear crystal water and yet when I want a drink it is not water." And that's when their great teacher who use to teach them about spirituality says, "This fountain you are looking at is called, "The Eternal Pool" it is surrounded by seven trees. Seven very tall trees, why seven trees?

There are seven worlds that Amyn, mentioned at the beginning but all seven worlds, are governed by the law of the eternal pool (more about this in the next chapter)

What is the law of the eternal pool?

The teacher says to them, that you are now going to have your progeny. You are going have more like yourselves. You are going to have children, and they will have their children, and their children until, this entire, forest that you see, will be covered by little ones and people like you. Therefore, it will be what would be called humanity, but you have to obey the law of the eternal pool. Look at the eternal pool what do you see?

Ibrahim says, "I see this pool flowing out of the earth and going back into the earth"

And the teacher said, "Yes, the fact is it flows" The law of the eternal pool is the law of flow. So, when you receive resources, when you receive wealth. If you receive wealth with this hand (right-hand) and you close your fist with this hand (left-hand) you cut yourself off from the eternal pool. You've killed the flow, you've built a dam. But if you leave this hand (left-hand) opened too then what you receive if you give a small amount of it away for others then you are maintaining the flow of the eternal pool with respect to resources.

Therefore, the great religions have what you call, "Tithing" where a small percentage of what you earn, sometimes it's five, eight or ten percent of what you earn and those are just numbers but by giving that small percentage away for the good of others we are completing the flow of the eternal pool therefore we always have access to that flow in our lives.

So, when we give, we are not doing anybody any favors, we are doing ourselves the greatest favour by been a part of the circle. It doesn't only relate to wealth. If you are a doctor and you have certain skills and without any direct gain to yourself, you help others with your skills then you have given, you have completed the cycle. If you have wisdom and someone comes to you for advice and you sit with him or her with compassion and give him or her advise then you have given of your knowledge, you have completed the cycle of the eternal pool. But the day you stop giving is the day you cut yourself from that pool, it's the day when your resources dry out. So, if you find yourself in a situation that is very difficult, you ask yourself, I am obeying the laws of the eternal pool?

Am I giving a part of myself towards the benefit of humanity; towards the benefit of others; towards the benefit of the planets, the trees, whatever; am I giving a part of myself so that I'm within that flow?

If the answer is yes then you shouldn't be in the situation you are in. if the answer is no then start looking, and start thinking about the eternal pool. And generally, you will find as long as that flow is maintained, remember this law applies to all the seven worlds the seven trees, so it's not just for our world.

So, if you can transcend the limitation of resources by using the law of the eternal pool. You end up in abundance and at the level of abundance is where the Origin lies. So, as we exchange monies every day, we buy, sell, this and that, those are all gifts for us to be able to complete our journey, but we don't look at it as that.

And Amyn is not saying, you go away tomorrow and give half your wealth away to somebody. He's not saying that at all. He's saying you have to be wise about it, to be wise about these things. You have to always ask yourself am I completing the cycle? And in the places where you are not completing the cycle that's where you find lacking in your life. And it is quite easy to fix but one has to think and start.

LOVE, BONDING & RELATIONSHIP – THE FOURTH HORIZON

The fourth horizon the Origin says to Maya, is the horizon of love, of bonding and of relationship. Sometimes when we love someone too much, they become a limitation and we become a limitation too to them because we cling too tightly to them.

And therefore, the limitation of that bonding, of that relationship, when we cling too tight becomes a horizon. If we are able to transcend the horizon of attachment, then we end up where there is limitless love and limitless love in where in lies the Origin.

There is a powerful meditation for learning to detach from clinging too tightly to everything that you love. To purchase this specific audio program, visit Amyn's website: www.amyndahya.com.

Now let it not be misconstrued that you must stop loving, what the Origin is saying to Maya, is do not cling tight to everything that you love because you stifle others at the other end, you stifle yourself and it becomes a horizon. And if you truly love someone, you must be willing, to set them free and let them go, that is the truest expression of love because if you are willing to give freedom, you will gain freedom.

And interestingly enough, if you are willing to let someone go that you dearly love. You actually gain them forever. So, the horizon of love, of bonding and of relationship is a very difficult horizon for us all to even consider transcending.

Remember at the end of that horizon lies limitless love and therein lays the Origin.

PRIDE & POWER – HORIZON NUMBER FIVE

The Origin goes to Maya, the fifth horizon that I have placed in this world is the horizon of Pride and Power. Pride is a major limitation.

How often do we hear people say, I can't do that because it's beneath me to do that, I'm above that, It's too low for me to consider doing A, B, C or D. Pride, Ego is a major horizon. It stops us from doing and sometimes, when that little voice in us says do this, when inspiration tells us do this, we say, no. It's below me to even consider doing that. So, pride and power are major limitations.

When we think about ourselves, we have to think about ourselves in 2 dimensions. We are like the speck of dust that is facing the universe. If you look at a speck of dust it's tiny, it's small, so we are the smallest of the small and yet, when you put your eyes into that speck of dust, what do you see? You see the entire universe, the largest of the large.

So, the smallest of the small is ultimate humility but when you recognize the largest of the large then there should be even greater humility, not pride.

One very useful exercise, perhaps to perform once a year is to take a walk in a graveyard. Just walk and read the tombstones and you will see for example: A C.E.O. of a 100-fortune company buried here, great accomplishments and then you will see next to him a Janitor, who perhaps cleaned the office building of this C.E.O. then you will see the gardener, who tendered his garden. So, these different situations from Kings to Slaves, they all end up lying together in that graveyard. That is a very sobering thought when you walk there to realize that what happened to these very powerful people? What was the meaning of their lives? Where did we all end up?

We all ended up completely equal. So that walk in the graveyard is a beautiful reminder for you, if you are suffering from Ego and Pride. A beautiful reminder of where you are going to end up as a physical form.

When you look at the work of the great prophets, look at prophet Mohammed, he received the revelation of Islam and he brought it amidst a world of incredible Power and Pride of the Koresh people. The Koresh people were the most economically powerful people in the region and he comes out with the revelation of Islam, talking about equality of all and worship to one God. Whereas these people believed in 100's of idols. He said, "This is the religion that has been revealed to me for the world at large and it is to be."

And these powerful people said, "It cannot be! We are the Koresh. We have ultimate power. We can stop you!"

What happened? What happened to the people who tried to stop him? We don't even hear about them, we don't even know who there are now anymore. What happened to the message he brought? It spread all over the world. A huge religion.

Look at the work of Jesus Christ, when he came, he came amidst the Romans, who were very proud and very powerful people. And he came with this beautiful religion, which was to transform humanity. What did they do?

They crucified him, they said, "Out of our power, we will destroy you." Did they really destroy him?

His work lives forever. What happened to the people who crucified him? We don't even know who they are today, they are totally irrelevant.

Look at Moses and look at Pharaoh, extremely proud and powerful man. Moses receive the revelation, brings forth the faith. The Pharaoh says, "I will destroy you, I will stop you, I am the ultimate power." What happened? Moses even parted the ocean and took his people across. His teachings, his works lives forever.

Those with Pride, Power and Ego, we don't even know anything about them today. So the horizon of Pride and Power is a major limitation that must be overcome. So when we find our Ego coming in the way, a walk in the graveyard is a very sobering exercise.

DEATH – THE SIXTH HORIZON

The sixth horizon is the horizon of death. It is when your life comes to an end. When we think about death, we think, I was born on 28th of June 1957 and my life comes to an end at a certain point in whatever year we pick. That is my birth and that is my death. Is that so? Wrong, that is not so. Each morning, when the sunrises we are born and each evening when the sunsets we die. Each day is a life in itself, this is why all the great religions teaches us about praying or remembering the creator at sunrise and sunset, why? Because sunrise is the birth and sunset are the end. Each day is a life. So, then we ask ourselves, so what did we accomplish in this, one, day?

Because tomorrow they may not be another day and life in itself is one day. And the total life of Amyn Dahay (as an example), however many years his going to live, is the sum total of those many births and deaths. So, each day is very important, when you think of the horizon of time and stretching time then think about each day as a life in itself.

So how do we transcend the horizon of death itself?

Well, death represents the end, so:

1. Is by living life to its fullest – Making each day a complete lifetime to its fullest.

2. Going back to the first law that the Origin gave to Maya, that I am the source of everything and that I am with your always.

If we seek the light of the Origin through meditation every day or even through our actions, through the way we live our lives, through meditation as an important key. If we discover the light, if we transcend the horizon, if we discover the light during this lifetime and we achieve ultimate freedom during this lifetime then what have we done? We have transcended death and we have gained eternal life while we are still in this body, while we are still encaged by the mind, we have gained eternal life. So, when our body perishes, it's just an event but we have transcended the horizon of death.

So very, very important, remember death is not the day you physically die. Every day is a life in itself!

BODY - HORIZON NUMBER SEVEN

The seventh horizon is the horizon of the body and as the Origin said to Maya, "I will engage you in a body that is completely limited to five senses" Maya started with 99 senses and she is down to 5. We all started with 99 senses and when we move on we gain them again, but we are down to 5.

How do we transcend the horizon of this engagement?

If you transcend the horizon of this engagement you gain freedom, ultimate freedom. Ultimate freedom is the purpose of Maya's birth.

When you think about your body, how well it functions. When you think about the Origin as a core and that we all have a connection to the Origin. Like a chord that connects us to our Origin. The roots that connects us to our Origin. Amyn, calls these roots, "SARAT" because it is a neutral word and it describes the connection between the body and its source. Some people use the word, "SOUL." Some people use the word, "SPIRIT." This connection is the path towards transcending the horizon of the body (engagement).

Let's look at it from a perspective of health. Let's say that we fall ill and one of us has cancer. You go for all your treatment, you go for chemotherapy, you took all these medications; and yet you are suffering, suffering, suffering and not coming out of it. You are not breaking out of it. We fall sick, we pop pills a, b, c and d at times e, f, g and h but we are still suffering, we are not getting better, why?

Because we are missing the essential tool – This illness has come to us, as a means to draw through those roots the power of healing from our source. Remember, the Origin said to Maya, I will always be with you. If we draw the power of healing from our source, our body gets well. The energies, flow within us, and when the energies flow within us, what happening? We are drawing from the limitless into the limited. When we achieve that we are healed. What has that whole process done? It has caused us to transcend the engagement that we are in. It has caused us to gain ultimate freedom.

Amyn shares an example of a lady; she was 42 years old, who had cancer in her two breasts and in her back. She came to Amyn for treatment. There was no hope left, she had a very short time to live and she said, "But I don't want to die, I want to see my daughter get married. Can you do something to help me, I'm willing to do anything"

So Amyn, talked to her about a Source – Do you believe you have a Source? She said, "Yes!"

Do you believe you have a connection to your Source? She said, "Yes!"

Okay, then what have you drawn from your Source to help you overcome this illness? She said, "Nothing!"

What do you call your Source? She said, "The Virgin Mary!"

Amyn said, "Great, let's start with the Virgin Mary!" And they went on to perform the healing meditation together, where Amyn helped her to draw that energy. Once she was able to draw it, she had such a great deal of inner strength and inner power that after that she was (within a four-week period) able to eliminate the cancer.

Today she works in a restaurant till 3am in the morning, if you saw her, you would not believe that this woman nearly died. That illness actually caused her to transcend that engagement through the body. The illness came to her as a gift. So, when we are suffering rather than feel really sorry for ourselves. We have to ask ourselves, why am I suffering this? When I was in Maya's stage did I choose this horizon to master? Did I choose this?

Yes, you chose it but now you have forgotten that conversation before we were born. From the moment we were born, it's over but if we build and use that illness as a means from which we draw the energies of the unlimited then we have transcended engagement. Then we have gained ultimate freedom then we don't need to come back again. Our journey is over, even when we suffer illness, we have to look at it from that point of view.

There are many ways for us to assess engagement and Amyn could talk for days on the subject – This is a good example of healing. Depression is another case and Amyn treats a lot of patients who have depression and they only ever need one treatment. Why? Because what is causing their depression? Either physical illness, pain or emotional stress or difficulty or business not working, or this is not working and the mind is saying, "Cannot be. Cannot be. Cannot be!" And they are depressed and as soon as they break free and travel up the roots that each one of us possesses into their Source and they receive the energy from the light. They are not depressed anymore, why? Because they have now had a flavor of "BE AND IT IS" as oppose to "CANNOT BE" and they heal very quickly. So, all our illness, come to us for a very good reason and sometimes they come to us as gifts if we are able to gain and learn from them to finish our journey. If we don't I bet you, you will be born again with the same problem until you finally learn.

FEAR – THE EIGHTH HORIZON

The eighth horizon is the horizon of fear. It's a big limitation. A lot of us are govern and driven by fear and yet fear is limited to time and space. It only exists within defined limits. If we transcend fear, we transcend to the level of limitlessness, Fearlessness that's where lie the Origin. Fear is a driving force that has destroyed and hurt so many, in Amyn's book, "Parables from the Origin" they are a wonderful story of a slave. He's a little boy, who was picked up as a slave in West Africa and he grows up in Europe and this story teaches a King who is about to trial him about how to overcome fear.

When you think of someone who has just been snatched from his home he must be really fearful. He sees his family disrupted right in front of his eyes and the slave said to the King, "Yes, in the beginning, anytime a leave moved, or a slight noise, I would be filled with fear but then I learned to embrace the unknown.

When you learn to embrace the unknown you become fearless.

A minute before, this boy was snatched from his home by the slave catchers; he didn't know one minute away what the slave catchers had in store for him. It had a disaster for him, it destroyed his family but, yet he learnt that the very next minute that lie ahead of him is still an unknown. So, if we learn to embrace the unknown we become fearless.

That which we fear is generally that which we anticipate.

There is a man and his son, who is lying in intensive care about to die and the doctor says, "He has two hours to live." This man, this poor guy is pacing up and down the hallway, fearing the moment when the doctor is going to say to him, "Your son is gone!" But if in the midst of that if he was able to overcome that fear – How could he overcome it?

If you bring that event, which you fear into the present moment. If you say, "I am afraid of my son dying in two hours then tell yourself he is died." Accept that event then this man would have spent those precious two hours with his son instead of pacing up and down the hallway because this is the most difficult thing that any human can face is losing a child or seeing a child suffer but if you brought that dreaded event into the present then those two hours would not have been lost. It could have been memorable hours between the father and the son, but they were gone.

Amyn Dahya often gives an example of a woman who had, had an affair and is being blackmailed by this blackmailer who goes after her for everything she owns, and she keeps paying and paying and paying. And her entire live, she dies of the stress and pain. Her entire life is lost due to that fear but perhaps if she had brought the dreaded event into the present and said, "My husband knows" faced her husband and told him, this is what has happened and let the chips fall where they do. Then those 15 years of total nightmare, she would have been spared from them. She may have continued with her marriage. She may have lost her marriage but those years, those precious moments that she came into this world to achieve where just lost in total fear. And that is something we all have to learn from and understand from this horizon of fear.

There was a very powerful financer in New York, who, use to run his organization with iron fist style. He would shred anybody who came in his way, who disagreed with him. He was so powerful and we all thought that this guy is really amazing. Until one day, the other side, the enemy, launched an attack and sued him for everything he had. Now he was faced with the prospect of losing everything he owned. What happened? He crumbled, this high and mighty fellow, the event hadn't even occurred yet. He hadn't lost the battle, but he was engulfed with fear and when you see fear like that you say, "My God, what happened to you?" He was such a strong guy engulfed with fear.

Until he came to the realization, okay, I have lost it all. I have lost my entire Empire. I have lost everything, and I have nothing left to lose now I'm going to take on this fight and he fought, and he won.

When you take the view, I have nothing left to lose, you go, and you fight and you win.

The Fatimid's use to be a very great civilizations in themselves but what was their main strengths?

At one time, there was a King who had come with a hundred thousand soldiers, who surrounded a Fort that belong to the Fatimid's. They were like a thousand people in that Fort.

So the King decided rather than slaughter everybody. He was going to send an emissary to deliver a message to say, "Surrender you are surrounded."

The emissary delivered the message and the commander of the Fatimid army said, I have one message for your King, he looks up and there is a soldier standing there and he say's to the soldier, "Jump off to your death" and the soldier just jumped and he landed and he died. He did not pause for a moment he just did it, he had nothing to lose.

When the emissary, so that this is the level of power this people possess, where they can give up their ultimate, which is their life itself. They are fearless people.

He went back to the King and said, "I think our hundred thousand people would lose to this guy's one thousand. We better turn around and go.

So, against all odds fearlessness is power, so we have to overcome the horizon of fear.

PHYSICAL DISTANCE – HORIZON NUMBER NINE

The ninth horizon is the horizon of physical distance, geography. We say, "I cannot do this I am limited because a, b, and c, this is far, I'm here it is there. Physical limitations of the way we find ourselves, and yet if you transcend the limitation of the physical spaces, and distances then you transcend to the level of the infinite. That which is not limited, and, therein lies the Origin.

You can seat today here and if you've been to South Africa, for example, in 5 seconds you can be in South Africa, and you can see and you can think and everything and you can be back. The power of thought.

Your power of thought can transcend all these physical limitations and barriers - And if you take that example above and extrapolate it, when we find ourselves physically limited, we are able to transcend this horizon. This is a relatively easy horizon to transcend.

Amyn, remembered when they were having their house built in the states. The architect came to him and he said, "What type of house do you want?"

Amyn replied by saying, "In order for you to build the house that I want you to build, you have to understand me. My first level of existence is the inner me (Amyn). What is that? To me it is humility, I am a humble person. My second level of existence is my body, so everything my body projects, must project humility in the way I act, in the things I do and in the way I dress. Then I go to my third level which is my home, and that too must project that which resides in me, which reflects in my body and now reflects in my home. So, you will build me a house that represents what I am. The house must also live in its fourth level of existence, which is it must fit into its environment. It can't be something that sticks out like a sore thumb (with tall pillars rising somewhere or with sharp edges), it's got to flow into the environment because I am humble, my body, my home into the environment, and the fifth is from the environment into the universe itself."

So that which begins with me projects itself right through to the universe. It's true about all of us. It's true about you and everyone else on this planet.

So, we talk of physical limitations, I am limited to a, b and c. No, we are not, we have dimensions to the limitlessness and we have to think that way to traverse. And when we cross that therein lies the Origin.

RITUALS, RELIGION, TRADITIONS, CUSTOMS – THE TENTH HORIZON

The final horizon is the horizon of rituals, religions, traditions and customs. Religions, rituals, traditions they can actually be a gateway to finding Oneness with the Origin but only if we understand their essence.

If we say, "This is the only right way, that is wrong, this is the only way." We are going nowhere, we are limited by those realistic traditions that we come from.

A good example is in the rain forest, in the Amazon and they have had no rain and these seven dancers. Danced around a rock praying for rain. But why do they do it? Because each one of them are each seeking rain, deep down in their essence and the seven of them get together and combine their force as they dance around seeking rain.

And through the power of their essence it rains. But if these dancers were too worried about their steps (my steps should be like this and I should take that step or that step in the dance) then there is no rain.

So, if they follow essence the result is there but if you get too bugged down with the how part you are limited. This is something that we all carry very strong thinking from childhood. So, it's not something we change but if we find ourselves limited by the how part and we are unable to achieve then we have to stop and ask ourselves, "Are we dancing around the rock and worrying about our steps or are dancing around the rock seeking from pure essence bringing down the rain? In our lives we may wish to bring something else.

And sometime these horizons of rituals, religions and traditions are ingrained. Our cultures are ingrained, traditions go from father to son, there're a source of enrichment and there make us what we are, they should be treasured but they should not be limiting forces.

We should be able to flow and think above them as well and that's where transcending that level takes us to the level of the essence, where in lies the Origin.

So, these are the 10 horizons, and Maya is about to be born. She has learnt these lessons and the Origin finally says to her, "When you are born you will forget this conversation. You will not remember this conversation. But within those 10 horizons and with all the tools I have given you, if you work with it you will gain ultimate freedom.

You and everyone on this planet called, "EARTH" have all had similar conversations with our Origin just like Maya did here but we just don't remember it. So, you have to think about it.

This is a huge thank you to Amyn Dahya for this inspiration he received and for putting it in such a way that all can understand from it and learn from it.

My hope and prayer are that this chapter on purpose will serve as an awakening of your soul so you can achieve your ultimate purpose and freedom in this lifetime.

SUMMARY PURPOSE – WHY ARE YOU HERE?

- Purpose is a composite of your passion, mission, profession and vocation. Something you love to do, the world needs it, you are great at it and you get paid to do it but even if you didn't get paid to do it. You would do it for free!
- "You know you are on the right path and on purpose if you are not put in a position to betray yourself."
- Everyone is on the right path you just sometimes get distracted and take a detour. And you don't manage situations well, as in you betray yourself and don't follow through on what you say you would do.
- To find your purpose ask yourself these questions – Who are you? What do you do? Who do you do it for? What do they need or want? And finally, how do they change as a result of what you do?
- To find your "WHY" ask yourself these questions. What drives you? What motivates you? And finally, what inspires you?
- I love my job, or I love what I do should become the standard not the exception.
- Doing something valuable gives you a sense of achievement and gives your life meaning.
- The 5 laws of the Origin (God, Creator, Source) or whatever you choose to call him are: 1. The Origin is the source of everything and he is with you always. 2. The Origin is Perfection itself. You cannot add or take-away from it. It's like energy it cannot be destroyed nor created it just is. Perfect!!! 3. The Origin is Uniformity, it permeates everything and its

everywhere at all times. 4. The Origin is pure Clarity. 5. The Origin is Unity (Oneness) connected to everything and everyone on the planet.

- The true purpose of our lives is to transcend the 10 limitless horizons in order for us to gain ultimate freedom (enlightenment) and union with our Origin in this lifetime.

- TIME-You will need to transcend the limits of time, so you can gain timelessness. Where there is no beginning and no end. You can achieve this by living every second to its fullest, to stretch every second to tis maximum.

- MIND – Your mind is a limitation in the sense that you can say, "BE AND IT IS" but you mind will trick you into believing that it, "CANNOT BE." You need to transcend the mind by remembering the 1st law of the Origin and meditate on it daily and secondly you can pay attention to your attitude is it one of I can do it or is it one of it cannot be done by me? Remember the Cactus story? Learn to be like the Cactus in attitude.

- RESOURCES – Resources are wealth, intellect, capabilities or skills. There is a limitation for you if you don't have it Here you are seeking abundance and the way to achieve that is by following the law of the eternal pool. Keeping the flow going by giving a part or portion of the resources you receive.

- LOVE, BONDING & RELATIONSHIP – This is only a limitation if you cling to tightly to things and people in our lives. This is one the hardest limitations to overcome. The way you can transcend this is by possessing the ability to let go and detach yourself from clinging too tightly to everything in your life including your children. Everything in your life is a gift for a designate period of time. If you truly love something or someone then you can let them go.

- PRIDE & POWER – Remember that this is a limitation of the Ego wanting control and power over another. You are the largest of the large and the smallest of the small. The way to transcend is to always keep the Ego in check and exercise humility. At least once or twice a year take a walk in the graveyard or cemetery and read the tombstones. *"Humility is not thinking less of yourself, but humility is thinking of yourself less." C.S. Lewis*

- DEATH – Each day is a life in itself. In the morning when you wake up (you are born) and at night when you go to sleep (you are dead). So, death is not the actual day that you physically die. To transcend death, remember to live each day to the fullest as if, it was your last because it may well be. Some people didn't make it to today. And secondly by remembering that the first law that the Origin is always with you and is the source of all thing.

- BODY – Your body is a limitation because you started off as an elevated soul with 99 senses and now you body is limited to only 5 senses. To transcend the body, we have to recognize our connection with the Origin. The Origin has a core and you are connected to this core via its roots. We all have our roots in this core. The root that connects us to our Origin is called, "SARAT" (SOUL OR SPIRIT). This is the path for transcending the limits of the body because we can all draw healing energy from this core (Origin) through this connection. You possess and have always possessed the power to heal yourself.

- FEAR – Fear is a huge limitation for many people and yet fear is only limited to time and space. Bring that which you fear into the present moment and it loses its power. To transcend fear, we have to become fearless and accept that which we fear by bringing it into the present moment, exposing it and revealing it so it no longer as a hold on us. Honesty is the best policy in this case. Let the chips fall where they may and move on with your life rather than wasting precious moments of life living in fear.

- PHYSICAL DISTANCE – Physical distance is Geography, it is a limitation because of the way we find ourselves and it can be transcended through the power of our thoughts. So that which begins with you must project itself from you right through to the universe.

- RITUALS, RELIGIONS, TRADITIONS & CUSTOMS – This are gateways for finding Oneness with the Origin but only if you understand their essence. No one, rituals, religions, traditions or customs is the right or wrong way or the only way. There are just one of the many ways to connect with the essence of your Origin.

"When you understand that what most people really, really want is simply to feel good about themselves, and when you realise that with just a few well-chosen words you can help virtually anyone on the planet instantly achieve this, you begin to realise just how simple life is, how powerful you are, and that LOVE is the key." Mike Dooley

"Do not go where the path may lead... go instead where they is no path and leave a trail."

Ralp Waldo Emerson

"To create reality focus beyond the outcome, as if it has already happened."

Gregg Braden

CHAPTER 6
UNIVERSAL LAWS – WHY DO YOU NEED THEM?

"There is no such thing as luck. Nothing ever happens by chance. Everything, good or bad that comes into your life is there as a result of unvarying, inescapable law."

Emmett Fox

WHAT IS UNIVERSAL LAW?

A law is the way things work, a process of doing things as in law and order as enforced by the police to protect the general public from harm or unscrupulous acts. Just as in politics there are laws, which are rules of government or rules of society that we all have to abide by or we face the consequences.

Similarly to these kinds of laws we have "Universal Laws," which are rules that govern our entire existence in life. Rules, that supports us, if we understand them and apply them appropriately into our daily lives. Laws, which allows the whole world to exist in the way it does.

The Laws are there to guide you as you explore and experience more of what life has to offer.

The challenge is that most people are not aware of what these Laws are and how to abide by them so that life is an effortless journey not one of struggles and heartaches.

You see, your life is just an experience and there is nothing bad or good about it. You just simply reap what you sow in life. It's all just an experience that you and I can learn, grow and share from.

On saying that they are consequences to every action you take, and those consequences are govern by Laws – Universal Laws.

WHY DO YOU NEED THEM?

Just like any government, society or community, without laws they are lost, confused and there is chaos. Law and order brings about principles and discipline.

You understand this law when it comes to your jobs and the physical applications of your job but as human beings our main challenges are mental in nature. They have no existence outside of themselves and when you or anyone is subjected to any degree of analysis you will discover that our problems are truly mental.

Hence the importance of understanding and applying the, "Universal Laws," in your life. It's your ability to learn how to use your innate powers unless you wish to be used by it.

"Always make it a point of moving forward in your mind, ever seeking to unfold your power of thought and to develop hidden possibilities. Learn to train the mind to clear an exact thinking."

Raymond Holliwell – *Working with the Law*

"The law is the uniform and orderly method of the Omnipotent God (our Origin)."

Thurman Fleet

One of my first mentors in personal development, Bob Proctor, who wrote the forward to Raymond Holliwell's book entitled, "Working with the Law," often quotes the statements of Dr. Wernher von Braun at his events and also mentioned this in the foreword of the book:

Dr. Wernher von Braun was a famous scientist, who was considered the father of our space program by many. He said that the natural laws of the universe were so precise that we have no difficulty today building spaceships, sending people to the moon and we can time the landing with the precision of a fraction of a second. He also stated these laws must have been set by someone. Bob agrees with him and would remark. The law is God's Modus Operandi; it's the way things happen.

In order for you to fully comprehend the Universal Laws of

the Universe you will discover, learn and explore the, "8 NATURAL LAWS OF THE UNIVERSE" even though there are numerous laws that govern our universe and planet; we will only be sharing with you in this chapter the core ones that will allow you to experience life in a more free, expansive and effortless way.

You and I are truly blessed to be alive right now in such a beautiful and magnificent world that operates on precise laws.

I suggest you make a firm decision right now to commit yourself to learning, understanding and applying the laws in your daily life. The discipline and effort you put forte here would be repaid back to you ten, hundreds or even a thousand-fold. Your life will be enriched with plenty and abundance, which has always been yours by virtue of being born, would be yours forever.

THE 8 NATURAL LAWS OF THE UNIVERSE ARE:

1. The Law of Cause and Effect
2. The Law of Perpetual Transmutation of Energy
3. The Law of Vibration
4. The Law of Relativity
5. The Law of Polarity
6. The Law of Rhythm
7. The Law of Gender and
8. The Law of the Eternal Pool

THE LAW OF CAUSE AND EFFECT

This could also be known as the law of thinking or the law of success.

The Law of Cause and Effect is denoted by this symbol C>E.

You already by the information give above that your whole universe operates in a precise and unique manner; it is able to do this because it is governed by, Universal Laws - And Cause & Effect is the main Law. The simple terminology means that for every action (cause) there is an equal and opposite reaction (effect). Meaning that as a result of doing x, y will occur.

In general terms our society tends to think of cause and effect as something outside their control. By this I mean something has happened to them, hence why they are the way they are. And I personally have fallen into this trapped many times in the past.

There is a big difference in saying: "The sunshine makes the flowers grow" Verses saying, "You made me mad."

The first example explains the natural laws of cause and effect, which I believe to be an extremely complex relationship with nature.

While the latter example, explains the human thinking of cause and effect. They believe that someone or something outside themselves is responsible for their emotional state. The effect of thinking this way is to give that person or thing all their, God-given powers. This assumes they have power over you, which they clearly do not have.

The main reason why this is so important cannot be overly

emphasised – It is vital because it brings people back to the realisation that they are actually responsible and in charge of their own emotional state of being. This understanding puts them back at cause by shifting them from the effect state of being.

So, the next time you hear yourself saying, "He or she made me mad, pissed off or angry" ask yourself how specifically did they do that?

The truth of the matter is that no one has the ability or power to make you mad, pissed off or even angry – You do that all by yourself based on your own internal interpretation of his or her behaviour towards you.

Unconsciously you have setup rules or association to external triggers that when you are exposed to them by way of seeing it, hearing it or feeling it you react by getting mad, pissed off or angry. It could be the way someone looked at you or the way you interpreted their look towards you, the way someone spoke to you or how their tone of voice sounded or the way someone made you feel or how they touched you etc.!

As human begins you have been endowed with the ability to think and this is your gift to act/impact upon the Universe and bring about the manifestation of your desires – And the results of this action and interaction is what is known as Cause and Effect; every thought is a CAUSE, and every condition is an EFFECT. You cannot have cause without a corresponding effect.

In today's society we have got our thinking reversed, rather than looking for the cause (thought, our thinking methodology) we focus on the effect (conditions, symptoms) and we try to cure the effect, and this might work temporarily in some cases but inevitably the effect returns because we have not addressed the cause.

If you have a headache rather than trying to numb the headache by taking a painkiller, why not ask yourself what is the cause of your headache (what happened? And what are your thoughts around what happened? And more importantly what and how are you thinking? In order to create this phenomenon, called headache.) You see focusing on the cause (thought) and changing the cause (thought) you can immediately eliminate the effect (condition).

It is said that for anyone to become successful they have to do things in a certain way. In order to do so, they must think in a certain way meaning the way you do things must and can only reflect the way you think about things.

So, for you to do things in a way that you want to do them then you will have to acquire the ability to think the way you want to think.

Most people think they think but they are not thinking only engaged in mental activities of yesterday and tomorrow. Real thinking is to think what you want to think regardless of the way in which things appear to you. In other words, think truth regardless of appearances.

What does that really mean? You see according to Wallace D Wattle in his book, "The Science of Getting Rich." Every person has the natural and inherent power to think what he wants to think, but it requires far more effort to do so than it does to think the thoughts, which are suggested by appearances. To think truth regardless of appearances is laborious and requires the expenditure of more power than any other work a person has to perform.

He goes on to say, "There is no labour from which most people shrink as they do from that of sustained and consecutive thought; it is the hardest work in the world. This is especially true when truth is contrary to appearance. Every appearance in the visible world tends to produce a corresponding form in the mind, which observes it. This can be prevented by holding the thought of the truth.

To look upon the appearance of disease will produce the form of disease in your own mind and ultimately in your body. Instead you must hold the thought of the truth, which is that there is no disease. Disease is only an appearance, and the reality is health.

To look upon the appearance of poverty will produce corresponding forms in your own mind. Instead, you must hold to the truth that there is no poverty. There is only abundance.

It requires power to think health when surrounded by the appearances of disease, or to think riches when in the midst of the appearance of poverty. But, he who acquires this power becomes a mastermind. He can conquer fate; he can have what he wants.

This power can only be acquired by getting hold of the basic fact, which is behind all appearances: that there is one thinking substance, from which and by, which all things are made.

Then, we must grasp the truth that every thought held in this substance becomes a form and that a person can impress his thoughts upon it so as to cause them to take form and become visible things."

This substance can be likened to the Origins first law of light, which is, The Origin is the source of everything in this world. Remember in chapter 5 the Origin said to Maya, "I will always be with you at all times."

The key thing to remember her is that this substance (Origin, God, Creator or Universal Intelligence or whatever you choose to call it) is the cause of everything and everyone on the planet and its first law is, the law of cause and effect. As man thinks so his he; in other words, you reap what you sow.

The cause of all prosperity, abundance, riches, success, affluence, material possessions, health, wealth and happiness is right thinking.

The cause of all poverty, lack, limitations, sickness, disease, separation, fear, resistance, loneliness, struggle is wrong thinking.

This is a very important Universal Law to understand and comprehend if one is to adopt the right way of thinking.

THE LAW OF PERPETUAL TRANSMUTATION OF ENERGY

This is a very powerful law that states all we are is "ENERGY" and energy cannot be created nor destroyed. It can only be transmuted from one form into another. Energy moves into physical form and the images you hold in your mind, most often materialize into results in your life.

What kind of images are you creating in your mind on a day-to-day basis? In other words how you think determines what pictures you create in your mind.

So, following on from the first law of cause and effect, there is one concept that you have to whole–heartedly believe in, is that the Origin is the source of everything in our world and that everything that is created comes from it. Everything!

Wallace D Wattle the author of The Science of Getting Rich put it succinctly in the following statements:

"There is a thinking stuff from which all things are made, and which, in its original state, permeates, penetrates, and fills the interspaces of the universe.

A thought in this substance produces the thing that is imaged by the thought.

A person can form things in his thought, and by impressing his thought upon formless substance, can cause the thing he thinks about to be created.

NOTHING can ever become SOMETHING, nor can SOMETHING ever become NOTHING. Substance can be converted, transmuted, and changed in a million ways, but it can never be destroyed. For example, if we plant an acorn in the soil, it will sprout forth a tree, Each year the tree will bring forth leaves in the spring and shed then in the fall. The leaves drop to earth and become a part of the fertile soil. The tree lives for a hundred years, dies, falls to the earth, and decays.

This decomposed timber slowly becomes part of the earth and it's hardened into peat and coal. The coal is mined and brought into the home as fuel.

Here it is consumed with fire and burned into ashes, and the heat units throw off are used to warm the home. The ashes are again cast upon the earth, supplying food to the soil, which finally natures another seed and causes it to sprout forth and become in time another great tree.

Following the cycle of the substance of a tree, we find it

changing form many times: we see it giving off gases, heat units, chemicals of many kinds, and yet if it were possible to be measured accurately, we would find that not one tiny part as been lost. All the supply there ever was, still is, and ever shall be, for nothing can ever be wasted or lost. There can never be a shortage in supply.

Because some people do not see abundance around them and do not enjoy plenty, is evidence that they do not understand or do not apply the law. In their blindness they say, that plenty does not exist, and so far as they can see, they may be right. But when they learn to see with their minds eyes, they will realise differently

And except from Working with the Law by Raymond Holliwell.

This law is evident in our lives every day and we have seen great people transform their lives and ordinary people transform their lives.

Take for instance the movie, "Trading Places," with Eddie Murphy. Most people in life are trading places all the time. The good news if you don't like what you have consciously or unconsciously created you can change it. Remember energy cannot be destroyed or created it just is. It can be transmuted from one form to another.

I personally took inspiration from a Ted-talk that was sent to me by Amyn Dahya about a young man called, Curtis "Wall Street" Carroll, who was talking about Financial literacy not been a skill but a lifestyle.

As an incarcerated individual, Carroll knows the power of a dollar. While in prison, he taught himself how to read and trade stocks, and now he shares a simple, powerful message that we all need to be more, savvy with our money.

Curtis "Wall Street" Carroll overcame poverty, illiteracy, incarceration and a lack of outside support to become a stock investor, creator and teacher of his own financial literacy philosophy.

Carroll grew up in Oakland, California surrounded by poverty. In 1996, at 17 years old, he committed a robbery where a man was killed. He turned himself in and ended up in prison with a 54-to-life sentence. While in prison, the stock market captured his attention, but he was illiterate. Finally motivated to learn, he taught himself how to read at 20-21 years old, and then he started studying the stock market. Carroll's role models changed from drug dealers and sports figures to Bill Gates and Warren Buffet. He wanted others to learn this new way of making money.

When Carroll arrived at San Quentin in 2012, he met Troy Williams, who helped him start the Financial Literacy Program. Together they created the philosophy F.E.E.L (Financial Empowerment Emotional Literacy) that teaches people to recognize how their emotions affect their financial decision, and how to separate the two.

Carroll's story is a true inspiration for me and there are many more stories like Carroll's in our world today.

The idea here is that you do not have to wait for a major disaster in your life to change your life. You can start today by thinking about what you want, picturing it the way you want it and take action towards that image and hold it with your will power until that image (energy) moves into physical form.

"Any idea that is held in the mind, that is emphasised, that is FEARED or REVERED will begin AT ONCE to cloth itself in the most convenient and appropriate form that is available."

Andrew Carnegie as given to Napoleon Hill

"Mind is the master power that moulds and makes and man is mind, and evermore he takes the tool of thought, and, shaping what he wills. Brings forth a thousand joys, a thousand ills. He thinks in secret, and it comes to pass. Environment is but his looking glass."

James Allen 1903 As a Man Thinketh

It is the law and you cannot escape from it, whether you are thinking negative or positive that energy will move into physical form. I'm sure you've heard of the saying, "Be Careful What You Wish For," because you might just get it.

I often say that, it is a miracle that the law is a perpetual transmutation of energy meaning nothing, is standing still you are moving all the time in one direction or another. Either you are creating or disintegrating. Either you are living or dying.

The challenge for most people is they are confused, they do not have any clarity as to what it is they really want. They want to be one thing one minute and another the next. This kind of thinking is the source of their doubt, fear, anxiety and the reason why they feel stuck in life. Have you ever felt that you take one step forward and then you find yourself taking 3 steps backwards? Life feels to you like a constant struggle. This is all because you haven't decided who you are and what you want in life.

Look around you and see those people who are achieving great results. They know who there are and exactly what they want and thereby find it very easy to think right and create the right images for themselves. Take sports for example: In Golf we have Tiger Woods, Rory Mcilroy and Dustin Johnson; In Tennis we have Roger Federer, Andy Murray and Rafael Nadal; In Football we have Lionel Messi, Cristiano Rolando and Neymar de Silva Santos.

This is not just in sports, but also in other areas like, business, education, health, politics and entertainment.

So it is vital that you have a goal and a purpose in life and that you know exactly what you want and who you are. This will allow you the freedom to think appropriately and with discipline and commitment you can create the life that you truly deserve.

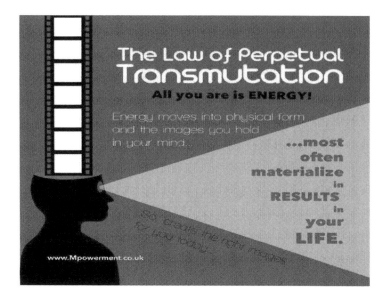

THE LAW OF VIBRATION

We hear a lot about the law of attraction and even movies (the secret or the abundance factor) have been made about it but yet it is a secondary law according to one of my earlier mentor (Bob Proctor). It's a secondary law to the law of vibration. So, in other words you could say the law of vibration precedes the law of attraction. You see words are loud noises and vibrations are feelings and feelings never lie and once there are felt. They have to be expressed through your physical body period.

The law of vibration states that everything vibrates, nothing rests and conscious awareness of vibration is called feeling. Your thoughts control your paradigms and therefore your vibrations. When you are not feeling good, become aware of what you are thinking then think of something pleasant. Go to a tranquil and peaceful place in your mind.

Remember your thoughts control your habits and your vibrations (feelings) therefore your vibrations will determine what you would attract to yourself, which will in turn create the condition based on your vibrations (feelings).

"Scientists tell us that thought is compared with the speed of light. They tell us our thoughts travel at the rate of 186,000 miles per second. Our thought travels 930,000 times faster than the sound of our voice. No other force or power in the universe yet known is as great or as quick. It is a proven fact, scientifically, that the mind is a battery of force, the greatest of any known element.

It is an unlimited force; your power to think is inexhaustible, yet there is not one in a thousand who may be fully aware of the possibilities of his thought power. We are mere babes in handling it. As we grow in understanding and in the right use of though, we will learn to banish our ills, to establish good in every form we may desire.

It is our power to think that determines our state of living. As one is able to think, he generates a power that travels far and near, and this power sets up a radiation (vibration), which becomes individual as he determines it. Our thoughts affect our welfare, and often affect others we think of. The kind of thoughts we register on our memories or habitually think attracts the same kind of conditions."

Raymond Holliwell – Working with the Law

Here's what you need to know and remember, your feelings count a great deal and in chapter four we talked a great deal about how to handle your emotions. The way you feel determines what you will attract so cleanse yourself of negative emotions by always expressing your emotions in the moment. Making sure you feel good at all times to attract good into your life.

THE LAW OF RELATIVITY

The law decrees that nothing is good or bad, big or small, until you relate or compare it to something in your life.

This has been the source of pain and heartache for many people because they look at their own lives and relate it or compare it to other peoples' lives. This could even be watching a movie on T.V or at the cinema, viewing other peoples' lives and wishing it was their own.

I have been guilty of this many times in my live until I came to this understanding that to compare your life to others is a dumb game and a stupid one at that. Are you comparing or relating your life to others? If you are stop it at once.

You see in every work of genius we see our own rejected thoughts – What you could have been if you applied yourself and weren't been lazy. What you could have been if you paid the price in terms of time, effort and money. What you could have become if you just had the discipline and courage to follow through on the things you said you would do. Does this sound familiar to you? It certainly does to me.

The truth of the matte is the only person you can truly compare yourself to, is yourself, because no two people are the same; Even if you are twins, you see one arrives before the other. They did not squeeze out of their mother's womb at the same time.

So looking at others achievements and comparing them to yours does not make any sense whatsoever. Even though physically we are all essentially the same with a head, two arms and legs, a face, body and we share the same nervous system.

If you get a cut, red blood would come out not green, so you can see that we are the same as human begins but our results are varying and very different depending on our applications of our mind power.

You and I have a very different upbringing, we come from different cultures, we attended different schools, colleges, universities (some didn't even attend university), so we have different educational systems, some of us even speak different languages, our parents are not the same they were brought up differently hence why they can only give us what they know how to. The list goes on.

Here's my suggestion to you rather than comparing or relating your life to others who you perceive are doing better than you just compare and relate to your current situation to your past situations.

As in, are you better today than you were yesterday? Are you better this week than you were last week? Are you better this month than you were last month? Are you better this year than you were last year? Are you better now 3 years later, 5 years later and 15 years later than you were 3 years ago, 5 years ago and 15 years ago? And for most people you will find that the answer is a resounding "YES YOU ARE BETTER!" So, give yourself a pat on the back instead of being so hard on yourselves.

Most people fail to recognise the blessings in their lives because they are so focused on what they are lacking and do not have in their lives. Learn to recognise and appreciate your blessing every single day. After all you did get up this morning and you are alive (that's a miracle and a blessing in itself) because some people never made it today. You did, be grateful for that.

Here's a thought – Practice relating and comparing your situations to situations much worse than yours and yours will always look, feel, sound, taste and smell good!

Did you know that if you owed nothing to anyone and you had a penny in your bank account in the black then you are wealthier than 95% of the population in the world because most people are in the red – And their bank balance is showing a minus (they living in negative equity), so if you a penny or more in the black then you are definitely better off.

The phrase, "The grass is always greener on the other side," and "It's okay for you but I was not born with a silver spoon in my mouth." referring to rich people's children, colleagues or friends.

Neither of these phrases or statements is true because when you dig deep and your analysis it you will find that no one ever got where they are without sacrificing something along the way.

You could say the law of relativity could also be the law of compensation, as in you reap what you sow. Or the law of sacrifice as in when you truly want something ask yourself what am I willing to give up getting?

All too often people want, what others have but are not prepared to do what others do to get what they want hence why they don't have it.

THE LAW OF POLARITY

The law of polarity states that there is a duality to all aspects of life. Everything has an opposite.

Hot versus cold, up versus down, good versus bad, left versus right, negative versus positive, heads versus tails, ugly versus beautiful, on versus off, poor versus rich, sad versus happy, failure versus success – And the list goes on!

Nature is all about abundance, balance and fairness, there is no competition. Life is not like a pie that you share, and someone get a bigger portion than another and eventually the pie rounds out. If everything is energy and it cannot be created nor destroyed but only transmute from one form to another. Then hear me when I say, there is no competition because there is more than enough to go round for everyone.

It is said, that if the whole worlds money, was shared equally amongst 7 Billion people on the planet, and even including an infant born today. Every single one would be a millionaire if not a multimillionaire.

The law is very practical as in if you look at a person and you say, "He or she is ugly," then it must imply that he or she must be beautiful too. The opposite always applies. I always share an exercise that I learnt from Dr John Demartini in his book, "Breakthrough" with my clients. It's always good to weigh up the pros and cons of doing anything or changing anything in your life.

For example, let's say someone wants to lose weight. Then they need to get a sheet of paper and divide it into columns. Label the first column 'Negative reasons for Being Overweight'. Label the second column 'Positive reasons for Being Overweight'. Go ahead and write down everything you can think of and at first this might seem a bit strange to you (especially finding something positive about being overweight) but at the end of it you will begin to see a pattern emerge and from there it's just an easy step to changing your behaviour.

Everything has an opposite meaning everything serves a purpose in our lives whether you are aware of it consciously or not. This exercise above will bring it to your conscious awareness.

I know personally, if I had erroneously judged my wife's past relationship and actions or if my wife had erroneously judged my past relationship and actions then we would not be together today and happily married.

There is always a benefit derived from the opposites above regardless of which one has shown up in your life. Or should I correctly say, which one you have created in your life, be it consciously or unconsciously. Here's what you need to learn, know and understand, is that these opposites are not different sides of two separate things. There are merely two sides of the same thing.

Let me explain, take a pound coin for example; you have heads or tails, right? The question is can you separate the head from the tail? The answer to that is, absolutely not. It's just two sides of the same thing and so are you. You cannot separate yourself from yourself. You have the tendency to switch between opposites and dip in and out of them at will.

The million-pound, question is, "Which one are you focusing on or which side of the coin are you dwelling on, or which side of the coin dominates your thought on a day to day basis?

Remember, "Where Focus Goes, Energy Flows" if you are not getting what you want to change your focus and look at the other side of the coin to start moving in a different direction and attracting something different. The height of insanity is doing the same things over and over and over again and hoping and wishing for a different result. Take it from me it's never going to happen, unless you decide, to change your focus and focus in the direction that you want in life.

THE LAW OF RHYTHM

The law of rhythm states that life is a constant flow of energy. The tides go out followed by the tides coming in. Night follows day. Good times follow bad times. Order follows disorder. Opportunity follows Difficulty. Recession follows Boom. Demand follows Supply. There is a cycle to everything in life just like the seasons. When you fully comprehend and appreciate this about life. You will find it more pleasant and happier to live in.

When you are on a down swing do not feel bad. Know the swing will change and things will get better. It's just the way life is. It's been that way for thousands of years and I promise you it's going to remain that way for thousands of years to come. It's the law of nature.

I kind of liken it to a roller coaster ride at the amusement park. You get on it and it seems to take forever to get you to the top. Then it drops you down with that feeling of euphoria and excitement and everyone is screaming and shouting enjoying the ride all the way down. Then you do it all over again, if you are someone who enjoys that sort of excitement. I know for certain the children would want to do it over and over again. You see your life is a bit like a roller coaster, whether you are in business for yourself or working for someone else. We all go through our very own personal roller coaster. The Key is not what happens to you because what happens to you happens to all of us. The key is how you react or respond to what has happened.

So, no matter what you're going through right now in your personal or professional lives. There are good times coming, think of them and expect them.

THE LAW OF GENDER

The law of gender decrees that all seeds have a gestation or incubation period before they manifest in form. You understand this law of life in relation to dealing with physical seeds. Then you must also understand that the non-physical seeds (ideas, goals, dreams) are just subject to the same law.

Take for instance when you plant a physical seed in the proper environment (fertile soil); you fertilise the seed and give it the energy (water) required for healthy growth. You keep the seed free of life-sapping weeds. Then you patiently wait as one who understands, with perfect belief, faith and positive expectation that the tiny microscopic seed will grow into a perfect physical form.

If you speak to a professional farmer or gardener, and asked them about, the gestation or incubation period, of any of their seeds or corps (tomatoes, potatoes, carrots or corns) they would tell you straight away. The have developed the awareness of exactly what period and time it takes for a physical seed to grow. This awareness came to them over time through observation and repetition of growing the same seeds or corps year in and year out.

I also strongly believe the day will come when we humans can readily predict the incubation and gestation period of a non-physical seed (idea, goal or dream). But until that time arrives you and I must guess.

Northcote Parkinson's Law states that, "Work expands to fill the time allotted for it."

So, when you set yourself a goal or an idea you want to

accomplish, just guess as to how long it will take you to achieve it.

We already know that if you are a woman and you were having a baby with your partner. From the day the baby is conceived, we know it takes roughly about 9 months of pregnancy to carry the baby to term before it is delivered – Bar any issues or complications. We also know that typically a premature birth is usually 2 weeks early but there are exceptions to the norm.

Now if the day arrives that you a have chosen and you have not reached your goal or idea, or there is no visible evidence that you will ever reach your goal or idea. Do not despair. It just means you chose the wrong time. Give yourself an extension of time and keep going.

Here's the golden rule, "Never change the goal or idea, change the time, change the plan of approach, but keep focused on the goal or ideal until you achieve it."

If you follow the golden rule, then you goal or ideal must manifest or create itself in physical form. It's the law.

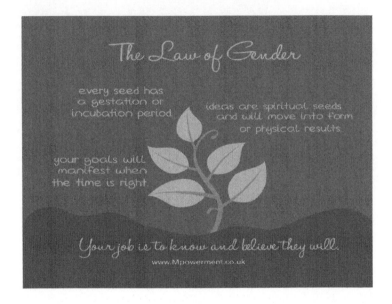

THE LAW OF THE ETERNAL POOL

The law of the Eternal Pool could also be called the law of Giving and Receiving.

The law is very simple to follow, for that which comes must also go to maintain its blessed flow. As in whatever gifts, talents, skills and abilities, incomes (these are resources) you've been blessed or provided with; the law is saying that you must be willing to freely give of that to others.

The reason for this is because generosity is a two-way street. For resources to flow freely, it must flow through open hands. One that gives and one that receives; in other words, if you receive with your left hand then you must give with of that which you have received with your right hand. This way you keep the eternal pool flowing.

242

The eternal pool was mentioned and referred to earlier in chapter 5 on Purpose.

Have you ever heard the saying, "Life is Giving!"

This is very true, but it is an area of total confusion for a lot of people. So, it requires study and understanding.

I believe it was Raymond Holliwell who wrote:

"In a state of limited understanding, we reason that we must get before we can give, and then we turn and walk in the same mental rut as before by reasoning that we must give before we can get; but in our lack of understanding, we continue to leave the "GETTING" idea foremost in our thought and we shut out the spirit of giving.

Giving is the first law of all creation. The attitude of getting is the law of life in a congested state, or in repressed action. As long as "GETTING" dominates a mind, that mind is in a paralysed condition, being limited in its action in accord with the fundamental law of creation.

The principle of life upon which this law is based is clearly written. It reads, "Give and it shall be given unto you, good measure, pressed down, shaken together, running over." Giving always precedes and predetermines the reception, whether you are giving your thought, your word, your service, or your deed.

Some folks may consider this law as a two-way law; that is, half the time you should be busy giving and the other half of your time you should be receiving. It is like the proposition of heat and cold; they are two sides to the same law. That is, if we concentrate upon cold and hope and pray to get heat, we are likely to freeze to death. What we must do is to give all our thought and effort towards building a fire or seeking that, which will create heat to warm us. If we concentrate upon receiving, not giving any thought or idea or desire to build upon, we, in like manner, may perish. The law says, "It is more blessed to give than to receive." And "as you freely give, you freely receive." Unless we are free to extend or give out our desire, our good, the, law will not have any pattern to work with. It cannot proceed to supply any need without a pattern. Many try to work the law backwards, and for that reason get little or no results, they say to themselves, "Well, after I get, then I will give." If you wish any good thing, you must first give some good to build upon."

So, if you want more money, give more money, if you want more love, give more love if you want more success give more success to others.

Often people say, "I have nothing to give," that is certainly not true and I used to be one of those people. It doesn't always have to be money it could be your time or just sharing your skills and ability with others to help them out of tricky situation. Now a word of caution here because how you give is very important and whom you give to is very important too.

Let me explain, if you are only giving to get then that is not the right way to give. You must give freely just like nature does. The sunshine gives you warmth but it does not ask for anything in return. The rain equally gives us water for our plants and crops, so we can have food to eat but asks for nothing in return. The moon shines bright to illuminate our paths as we drive at night without asking for anything in return. You must also give according to how nature gives – Freely and as the law states it must come back to you or more importantly helps to keep you in the flow.

This is where true abundance is discovered and maintained, through giving.

SUMMARY UNIVERSAL LAWS – WHY DO YOU NEED THEM?

- "Universal Laws," are rules that govern our entire existence in life. Rules, that supports us, if we understand them and apply them appropriately into our daily lives. Laws, which allows the whole world to exist in the way it does.

- It's important to have these laws, just like any government, society or community, without laws they are lost, confused and there is chaos. Law and order brings about principles and discipline.

- There are numerous laws guiding our universe and here I would like to share with you the 8 Natural laws of the Universe that I consider to be most valuable to learn, understand and apply daily.

- The Law of Cause and Effect – Whatever you send into the Universe comes back. Action and re-action are equal and opposite. So, say good things, to everyone, treat everyone with total respect and it will all come back to you. Never worry about what you are going to get, just concentrate on what you can give and give it with all you might and ability.

- The Law of Perpetual Transmutation of Energy – All you are is ENERGY! Energy moves into physical form and the images you hold in your mind, most often materialise in results in your life. So, create the right images for you today.

- The Law of Vibration – Everything vibrates nothing rests and conscious awareness of vibration is called feeling. Your thoughts control your paradigms (Habits) and your vibrations. When you are not feeling good, become aware of what you are thinking about then think of something pleasant. Go to a tranquil and peaceful place in your mind.

- The Law of Relativity – Nothing is good or bad, big or small, until you RELATE/COMPARE it to something in your life. Practice relating/comparing your situation to something much worse and yours will always look, feel, sound, taste and smell good!

- The Law of Polarity – Everything has an opposite: Hot or Cold, Up or Down, Good or Bad, Left or Right, Negative or Positive, Heads or Tails, Ugly or Beautiful, On or Off, Rich or Poor, Sad or Happy. Constantly look for the good in people and situations. People love compliments and the positive idea in your mind. When you find it, tell the other person? It makes you feel good about yourself for doing so. Remember, good ideas – good vibrations.

- The Law of Rhythm – The tides go out, night follows day, good times follows bad times, order follows disorder. When you are on a down swing, do not feel bad. Know the swing, will change and things will get better. It's just the way life is, so no matter what you're going through right now. There are good times coming, think of them and expect them.

- The Law of Gender – Every seed has a gestation or incubation period. Ideas are spiritual seeds and will move into form or physical results. Your goals will manifest when the time is right. You job is to know and believe they will.

- The Law of the Eternal Pool – The Eternal Pool provides all the resources of life, from health to wealth, to wisdom and more. Its law is simple to follow for that which comes must also go to maintain its blessed flow. Generosity is a two-way street. For resources only flow through open hands, one that gives, and one that receives. Discover abundance through giving.

"Goal setting is an intellectual exercise, goal achievement on the other hand is a lawful process. When you understand and apply the laws of the universe taught here in this book, achieving your goals will become easy, natural and effortless."

Tosin Ogunnusi

SEVEN ETHICS OF LIFE:

Before you Pray—Believe

Before you Speak—Listen

Before you Spend—Earn

Before you Write—Think

Before you Quite—Try

Before you Hate-Love and

Before you Die—Live

CHAPTER 7
IDENTITY – WHO ARE YOU?

"Promise yourself to be so strong that nothing can disturb your peace of mind. Look at the sunny side of everything and make your optimism come true. Think only of the best, work only for the best and expect only the best. Forget the mistakes of the past and press onto the greater achievements of the future. Give so much time to the improvement of yourself that you have no time to criticise others. Live in the faith that the whole world is on your side as long as you are true to the best that is in you!"

Christian D. Larson

What is Identity?

Identity is the labels you give yourself based on past conditioning. It's a funny thing these labels that most people share, 90% of them are negative self-talk.

If you are being honest how often have you heard friends, colleagues and loved ones or perhaps yourself, say the following words:

"I'm stupid;" "I'm not very clever you know;" "I have a bad memory, I'm always forgetting things;" "I'm not good enough;" "That's a crazy idea, there's no way it's going to work;" "I'm ugly;" "Money is the root of all evil;" "It's better to be poor than rich and miserable;" "I'm not strong enough, I'm too weak; "You can't teach an old dog new tricks"; "I can't do that, it's too complicated for me;" "I'm too old to learn;" "I'm too young, too fat, too thin;" "My bum/boobs/arms/legs is too big, too small etc."

Are you beginning to get the general idea? I'm sure if you are being brutally honest with yourself you may have uttered one of these negative self-talks which are just labels that you have associated or linked with your identity of who you think you are.

Now you might be asking so what Tosin, why is it important what I call myself at least I'm not saying it about anyone else?

Here's the thing, what you say to and think of about yourself is far more powerful and potent than anything anyone else can say about you. And when someone labels you or gives you an identity by calling you names or using one of the above negative self-talks and you get upset and angry about it! Then it is more likely that you yourself have accepted whatever it is they said to you, for it to affect you because you believe it to be true yourself – Remember this, "No one can make you feel inferior without your consent." This is one of Eleanor Roosevelt's, famous quote.

If you didn't believe it then you wouldn't give it any energy, focus our attention but if it affected you emotionally in anyway then perhaps unconsciously or consciously in some cases you have allowed other people's opinions of you to become your own reality.

A good example to illustrate this point was a story I heard about the amazing Tony Robinson, he was conducting an event for Black people about 3000 of them in a room. I believe it was in aid of Black History month and as soon as he was introduced to the audience he said, "How are you all doing, "NIGGERS?" And before he could utter another word the whole entire room erupted into an outright rage of anger and foul language towards Tony. If Tony had been a normal guy on the street then he would have been punched repeated in the face but for the fact he had security and he's not normal in every sense of the word because he's a giant of man, a freak of nature I call him but I mean that in a positive way – The guy is huge! Built like a giant.

Anyway, I digress, Tony let the rage settle and when everyone had calm down a little he proceeded to tell them that 80% of the room that went into an uncontrollable rage were still living in slavery and bondage from the past because all he did was use a word, "NIGGER" and that triggered off some old wounds that caused majority of the room to go into a wild rage. Why would you do that? It didn't make any sense at all and the irony here is that most black folks call themselves that all the time and it's okay for them to use the word but no other people especially Tony Robins why? Because he his white? Not at all, the only reason is the association/link that they have attached to the word based on the past atrocities that had been committed in the days and times of slavery. This story clearly shows that many of us have not moved on from the past and we have linked the word, "NIGGER" to our identities.

As soon as Tony explained is reasoning and thinking behind using the word as a way of teaching and sharing an important point to them around Incantations the whole room where now in agreement and saw the errors in their ways – You see people can call you names or all manner of things, but you are in charge of how you respond to them. Remember, it's just an opinion and everyone is entitled to their own opinion - Just don't get hooked by it or on it.

Now back to why you should be very careful what you say to yourself and others on a daily basis – Did you know that you only have to repeat a negative self-talk or label 5 times to yourself before it takes hold and becomes an Identity that you now live by a bit like a negative affirmation if you like. For instance (I'm am weak), you only have to repeat that 5 time and you become it instantaneously.

Can you change your Identity? Yes, you can absolutely, mainly by affirm the opposite of your negative self-talk or labels e.g. "I'm weak becomes I'm strong."

This works very well but I want to talk about something Tony Robins mentioned earlier, "INCANTATIONS"

What are Incantations?

They are similar to Affirmations but much more powerful in changing, re-wiring and re-conditioning your old identities with a brand new one. It's a series of words combined in a positive way to boost your state of mind and give you total confidence and certainty towards doing the things you want to do and accomplish. These series of positive words are repeated out loud daily for at least 10, 15 or 20 minutes every day.

Initially, to get you going you repeat it for 90 days and during these 90 days your incantations will become an active part of your neurology hence why it is more potent than just affirming a word – More about that later.

Now I want to share with you is why this is so important for you to do. Just as there are positive incantations you also have "InCan'tations," too. These are the words that form your negative identity. You see you can't get rid of an incantation, what you must do instead is replace it with a positive one.

It's important for you to do this because your unconscious mind takes everything about you personally; meaning you can't say, "I'm just teasing or joking at myself." And knowing better will never make you better. You must speak that which you wish to become into existence because here's the truth about you:

"What you consistently say to yourself you will become, what you consistently say to yourself you will create and what you consistently say to yourself you'll find in your experience."

It's pretty simple to understand, what you say and speak to yourself over and over and over and over and over and over and over and over and over again becomes the operating system of your brain, which, in turn goes to work on your behalf to produce the outcome you have programmed it with – This is the reason, why, you've got to do it more consciously now.

So, whichever way you look at it, "This is your Paradise (Heaven) and this is your Nightmare (Hell) right here on planet earth.

The secret is to create a new identity that will support and assist you in achieving your goals and purpose in life based on your values. And the more powerful your emotional state is when you read out loud your new identity or incantation, as Tony would call it; the more powerful the conditioning will be.

So, rather than trying to do something using your will power. Just by reciting your incantation daily, it will put you into the desired state or the right mind-set to deliver your outcome. It will put you in the state you need to be in, which makes doing the thing you need to do automatic.

You literally live, breath and totally embody your incantation or new identity so that you become it.

There are a few distinctions here that you need to adhere to, strictly, in order to make your incantations really work for you. Remember Incantation/Affirmation without discipline is the beginning of insanity.

1. EMOTIONS
   Your new identity or incantations are just some random words on a piece of paper. You have to make it real by believing it and getting emotionally engaged with it at all levels; spiritually, mentally and physically. The way you do this is by emotional intensity. Play your favourite music and as your music plays recite out loud your incantation using your physical body to generate some intensity and totally embody what you are saying out loud not just some empty words in which you are affirming.

2. CONSISTENCY

The mother of all skills is repetition and it's no
different with your new identity or incantation you
need to internalise it and externalise it meaning know it
inside out. You see to condition it into yourself you
need to repeat it over and over again, you need to write
it out over and over again. Consistency in this instance
is real Power! So, schedule it in your diary and do it
daily consistently preferable at the same time each day
or while you run or exercise in the gym. Make sure you
are incanting for at least a minimum of 10, 15 or 20
minutes per day.

3. POETIC

You need to make your new identity or incantation
rhythmical that is certain words need to rhyme
together as if you are reciting poetry. So, as you speak
it out loud it almost sounds like a song.
For example: "I am getting better and better every day
in every way." "I am sillier than ever, louder than ever
and simply outrageous." "I am totally healed and
getting stronger and stronger every single day in every
single way." "I am a total expression of health and
vitality."

4. REWARD

Find creative ways to reward yourself for taking daily
and consistent action towards your new identity or
incantation.
Common rewards for me are Cinema time; A round of
Golf or movie, treat at home. This will keep you
engage, motivated and on track. A reward is like
something to look forward to for putting the effort in.
Celebrate your successes.

5. SAMENESS

This is a key vital point. Keep the same incantation or new identity going until you have achieved it. Then move on to a new and bigger one. Too often people start with one incantation and they keep changing it every other day or every week or monthly without ever achieving anything. The goal is to set your new identity or incantation so big it juices, excites and scares you all at the same time that you are willing to work hard for it in order to make it a reality in your life.

Now you can make minor changes to make it read and sound and feel well to you, but I would say maximum 3 minor tweaks a year. I used to change my every year as I achieved them with relative ease. So this year (2017), I decided to go beyond my wildest dream and created a masterpiece, which I'm going to keep incanting until I achieve it. It's become my daily mantra and I suggest you do exactly the same.

6. ACCOUNTABILITY

Make a commitment to a coach, mentor, friend or buddy that will hold you accountable for writing down and reciting your incantations and new identity daily. This will allow you to create a habit very quickly – And give your accountability partner the authority to whip your butt if you do not follow through on your commitment. So, what I mean is they must be a punishment for not following through just as you reward yourself for following through on your commitments.

The best way that I have found to do this is to make a list of things you would have to do and perform if your partner does not follow through on their commitments. Seeing that human beings would do more for others than for themselves this now puts you under pressure to deliver because if you don't then

your coach, mentor, friend or buddy is going to be doing the punishment not you. Ouch!!!
They are not going to be happy with you if you continuously fail to deliver on your promise.
So, for instance if you do not write and recite your incantation for 15-20 minutes a day then your accountability partner has to perform 50 press ups for each day that you fail to do it.
This is a really good way to get you focused, disciplined and committed to your new identity and incantations.

Here I want to share with you my new identity and how you can create your own using, "The A.N.V. New Identity Generator."

MY NEW IDENTITY

I Oluwatosin Ogunnusi **AM** Adventurous, taking calculated risks fearlessly, I'm Articulate, Caring, Cheerful, Colourful character, Confident, Courageous, Creative, extremely Energetic, Flexible, Funny, Playful, Intelligent, Inspiring, Loving, Positive, Sincerely Grateful for all that has been provided for me and my family thus far…

AND I'm Oneness connected to everything and everyone on the planet, a goal Achiever, a published Author of 8 bestselling books, a Billionaire creating earning capacities for millions of people around the world, a Catalyst, an Instrument of God, a Healer, a Leader, a Mentor/Role model to others, a great Family man, an Expression of pure Health & Vitality, a Champion, a roaring Tiger from within, a born Orator, sharing the Voice of the Universe to Co-Create destinies…

THAT Advises, Strengthens, Experiments, Appreciates life… and all that she has to offer, by Gathering and Applying information for Knowledge, Wisdom and Light; in order to deliver high standards of training, which in turn allows me, you and others to create and grab opportunities that is all around us. I protect others, heal others and inspire others to, Give More, Be More, Do More and Have More in their lives. I am (MAD) because I Make A Difference and as a result, I'm contributing to making this world a better place to live in. I always play full out, by tapping into my full potential every single day – As I take full responsibility for my own life.

This is who I am!!! Who are you?

What is "The A.N.V? New Identity Generator?"

This is a cool process that I take my personal coaching clients and audiences of our Flagship event "Time 2 Break Free Boot-camp" through, to assist them in coming up with their own new identities and daily incantations.

It's a process of combining Adjectives, Nouns and Verbs together in a unique way.

Create Your New Identity
Sheet 1 – Adjectives

Tick between three and five of the words below – the words that jump out to you the most...

☐ Adorable	☐ Elegant	☐ Magnificent
☐ Adventurous	☐ Energetic	☐ Outstanding
☐ Aggressive	☐ Exciting	☐ Plain
☐ Alert	☐ Fabulous	☐ Playful
☐ Amazing	☐ Faithful	☐ Positive
☐ Articulate	☐ Fancy	☐ Powerful
☐ Attractive	☐ Flamboyant	☐ Powerful
☐ Awesome	☐ Flexible	☐ Precious
☐ Beautiful	☐ Flirty	☐ Sexy
☐ Breathtaking	☐ Fulfilled	☐ Shiny
☐ Bright	☐ Funny	☐ Sincere
☐ Brilliant	☐ Graceful	☐ Sparkling
☐ Caring	☐ Grateful	☐ Spectacular
☐ Cheeky	☐ Handsome	☐ Spotless
☐ Childlike	☐ Happy	☐ Trustworthy
☐ Clean	☐ Humorous	☐ Unique
☐ Clear	☐ Inspiring	☐ Wicked
☐ Colourful	☐ Intelligent	☐ Wonderful
☐ Confident	☐ Joyful	
☐ Courageous	☐ Kind	
☐ Creative	☐ Light	
☐ Curious	☐ Loving	
☐ Cute	☐ Loyal	

Create Your New Identity
Sheet 2 – Nouns

Tick between three and five of the words or phrases below
– the ones that jump out to you the most...

- ☐ Achiever
- ☐ Angel
- ☐ Author
- ☐ Authority
- ☐ Billionaire
- ☐ Catalyst
- ☐ Cause
- ☐ Champion
- ☐ Coach
- ☐ Comedian
- ☐ Commander
- ☐ Creator
- ☐ Dancer
- ☐ Destiny forger
- ☐ Director
- ☐ Earth
- ☐ Expression of health
- ☐ Family
- ☐ Father
- ☐ God
- ☐ Goddess
- ☐ Grandfather
- ☐ Grandmother

- ☐ Guru
- ☐ Healer
- ☐ Heart
- ☐ Instrument
- ☐ Kiss
- ☐ Leader
- ☐ Legend
- ☐ Man
- ☐ Manager
- ☐ Maverick
- ☐ Memory
- ☐ Mentor
- ☐ Millionaire
- ☐ Mother
- ☐ Mother nature
- ☐ Motivator
- ☐ Mountain
- ☐ Musician
- ☐ Ocean
- ☐ Oneness
- ☐ Orator
- ☐ Playground
- ☐ Prince

- ☐ Princess
- ☐ Professional
- ☐ Professor
- ☐ Representative
- ☐ Role model
- ☐ Sculpture of souls
- ☐ Sex machine
- ☐ Spark
- ☐ Star
- ☐ Student
- ☐ Summer
- ☐ Supermodel
- ☐ Superstar
- ☐ Teacher
- ☐ Team
- ☐ Tiger
- ☐ Universe
- ☐ Voice
- ☐ Woman

Create Your New Identity
Sheet 3 – Verbs

Tick between three and five of the words or phrases below
– the ones that jump out to you the most...

☐ Accelerates

☐ Activates

☐ Administers

☐ Advises

☐ Amuses

☐ Analyses

☐ Anticipates

☐ Appreciates

☐ Arranges

☐ Creates

☐ Creates opportunities

☐ Delivers high standards

☐ Demonstrates

☐ Develops

☐ Discovers others

☐ Elevates others

☐ Encourages

☐ Entertains

☐ Experiments

☐ Feeds

☐ Focussed

☐ Gathers information

☐ Grabs opportunities

☐ Guides

☐ Heals people

☐ Inspires Light

☐ Inspires others to do more

☐ Investigates

☐ Leads

☐ Lights the next torch

☐ Loves

☐ Maintains

☐ Makes a difference

☐ Makes dreams come true

☐ Makes the world a better place

☐ Motivates others

☐ Opens doors

☐ Persuades

☐ Plays full out

☐ Powerful

☐ Protects others

☐ Provides

☐ Recommends

☐ Reorganises

☐ Rocks

☐ Runs

☐ Saves the planet

☐ Shares

☐ Spreads

☐ Stimulates

☐ Strengthens

☐ Stretches

☐ Succeeds

☐ Supplies

☐ Supports others

☐ Sybolises

☐ Systemises

☐ Takes ownership

☐ Takes responsibility

☐ Taps into potential

☐ Travels

☐ Understands

☐ Unlocks

☐ Upgrades

☐ Utilises

Create Your New Identity
Sheet 4 – My New Identity

Now it's time to create your new identity from the words you have chosen. We do this by writing them out as follows:

I (your name) am (list your adjectives here) and (list nouns here) that (list verbs here).

For example:
"I John Smith, am funny, inspiring, energetic, intelligent, flexible, happy and oneness, a mentor, a leader, a healer and a dancer that protects others, inspires others to do more, makes a difference, taps into my full potential, plays full out and takes full responsibility for my own life."

Now it's your turn:

I _____ am _____

and _____

_____

that _____

_____

This is your new identity – Say it with pride!

TAKE ACTION
Be the person you want to be. To really feel the benefits of your new identity, say it out loud to yourself in the mirror EVERY day for 90 days.

Now it's your turn to create your own incantation and new identity that will support your growth and existence.

Once you are done, I would love to hear from you by emailing (info@mpowerment.co.uk) over your incantation or posting it on our Facebook page: www.facebook.com/mpowermenttosin.

Here below is a collection of my favourite incantations that has formed part of my morning rituals.

Some of them have been collected from mentors and others have been adapted and some I have just read in books with unknown authors but together they represent my Holy Grail and daily ritual.

You are free to use them as you will or adapt them in any way that you see fit. Enjoy:

OATH OF MANIFESTATION

I Oluwatosin Ogunnusi accept and receive unexpected good, unexpected money, unexpected love, unexpected kindness, unexpected generosity, unexpected offers, unexpected prosperity coming in unexpected ways from unexpected places in my life and the life of others. I am constantly guided, and boldly empowered, to receive the lavish abundance of the Universe! I accept the Principle that abundance and prosperity have already been given to me. My acceptance makes it real and opens the space for manifestation to rush in! I open wide the doors of my consciousness to receive and to give! It IS done now!

Through this Oath of Manifestation ALL things are possible! I declare, absolutely that I live in a friendly Universe that is always providing for me. I feel it powerfully happening now! I open to receive more abundance, and to give more abundance, than I have ever experienced before! I can afford anything I desire! In fact, I am so prosperous I need never worry again! I am grateful for all that I already have, and grateful for all that I am ready to give! I keep myself lifted in high consciousness, no matter what the appearances are! God is all there is! I let the God-times roll! And so IT IS!

The Secret Book by Rhonda Byrne

HEALING INCANTATION

I am secure in the soles of my feet, I am supported in the base of my spine, I am strong in the naval, I am calm in the solar plexus, I am open in the heart, I am kind in my throat, I am free right from the centre of my forehead.

I am worthy from the top of my head, I am enough far and wide and I am totally healed in my entire body.

All my bodily functions work according to how they should every single day!

I am getting stronger and stronger and getting better and better in every single way, today!!!

Adapted by Tosin Ogunnusi

WEALTH INCANTATIONS

GOD's wealth circulates in my life. His wealth flows to me in avalanches of abundance, all my need, desires and goals are met instantaneously by infinite intelligence and I give thanks for all my good now and for all of GOD's riches for I'm one with GOD and GOD is everything.

By Tony Robbins

PERSONAL INCANTATIONS

Now I am the Voice.

I will lead, not follow.

I will believe, not doubt.

I will create, not destroy.

I am a Force for Good.

I am a leader.

Defy the odds!

Set new standards!

Step Up! Step Up! Step Up!

Now I know I'm good as Gold and life is not a test. I celebrate my accomplishments but I realise they are not me. As I love myself, I'm all that I ever need to be.

By Tony Robbins

CERTAINTY FOR WORK INCANTATION

I now command my subconscious mind to direct me in helping as many people as possible today. To give me the strength, the emotion, the persuasion, the humour, the flexibility and whatever it takes to show these people and to get these people to change their lives now – By making a decision to attend one of our events (**T2BFB** or **EAIT** or **SPWI** or **ECCT** or 12 month **1:1 MENTORING** with myself) or all of them.

Adapted by Tosin Ogunnusi

THE WINNER'S CREED

I am a fighter. Every problem in life, every struggle, is merely a game for me to enjoy and win. I am an intelligent fighter, using the brain and instinct for survival that was passed on to me by countless generations of ancestors a genetic, gift my inheritance. I am a winner, because I refuse to accept defeat: I can only be defeated if I give up, which I never shall. Every success makes me stronger. Every experience makes me wiser. Every new fight gives me another chance to win. And I enjoy winning.

To the timid, the approaching battle looks worse than to the fighter. It is magnified by fear, but reduced and overcome by courage. I begin and finish a winner, because I know that all I have to do is to stay strong and keep fighting, until I tire out the opposition.

Merely being prepared and willing to fight is my greatest asset.

I shall always strive to be a winner. *Unknown Author*

I WILL WIN - The die has been cast I've stepped over the line. The decision has been done the destiny's, been determined. I will no longer vacillate. I will no longer vacate. I will no longer listen to, listen at or listen in on losing. I will not be defeated, dejected, diluted or detoured. I will no longer navigate with the needle of negativity. The direction's been decided, the trail to be tried. The destiny directed the future forged. I will not be pulled on, pulled in, pulled down or pulled out. I won't back up, back down or back away or back off. I won't give in, give out or even give way to defeat. I no longer will meander in the maze of mediocrity. I will no longer conform to the cancer of can't. I now will confirm the condition of can. I will, probe, the possibilities, pick the probabilities. I will focus on the fire and heat it even hotter. I will never give up, let up, set up or shut up on success. I am reaching for the ring, pulling on the power. I've quit wishing, hoping, wasting and whining. I now will aggressively gear into the word go. And I am determined to dare to do till I drop. I will withstand the whining winds of defeat. And I will be powerfully persistent, consistent and insistent. To get out of life what I truly deserve because I am willing, I am waiting, I am worthy and I understand the only defeat is from within. I now know that beyond any shadow of the cloud of doubt, there is no shadow, there is no cloud, and there is no doubt. **I WILL WIN!!!**

Unknown Author

AWAKE & ALIVE

I'm showing up every day in good spirit and health, going after my hearts desires and goals by being myself every second, minute and hour of every day. I'm happy getting things wrong because it means I'm learning and in time will eventually get it right.

I live for every moment in the **"NOW"**... I'm constantly in flow and in the zone... Accepting others for who they are being and I've stopped judging others and being right all the time, and as a result I'm sillier than ever, loving myself unconditionally, by stepping beyond courageously, and dancing wildly, in complete amazement, at my co-creating, abilities in connection with my Origin. I can't believe it I'm completely, awake and alive!!!

Adapted by Tosin Ogunnusi

STATEMENTS OF ABUNDANCE CONSCIOUSNESS

1. God is lavish, unfailing Abundance, the rich omnipresent substance of the Universe. This all-providing Source of infinite prosperity is individualized as me – the Reality of me.

2. I lift up my mind and heart to be aware to understand, and to know that the Divine Presence I AM is the Source and Substance of all my good.

3. I am conscious of the Inner Presence as my lavish Abundance. I am conscious of the constant activity of this Mind of infinite Prosperity. Therefore, my consciousness is filled with the Light of Truth.

4. Through my consciousness of my God-Self, the Christ within, as my Source, I draw into my mind and feeling nature the very substance of Spirit. This substance is my supply, thus my consciousness of the Presence of God within me is my supply.

5. Money is not my supply. No person, place or condition is my supply. My awareness, understanding and knowledge of the all-providing activity of the Divine Mind within me, is my supply. My consciousness of this Truth is unlimited; therefore, my supply is unlimited.

6. My inner supply instantly and constantly takes on form and experience according to my needs and desires, and as the Principle of Supply in action, it is impossible for me to have any needs or unfulfilled desires.

7. The Divine Consciousness that I am is forever expressing its true nature of Abundance. This is its responsibility, not mine. My only responsibility is to be aware of this Truth. Therefore, I am totally confident in letting go and letting God appear as the abundant all-sufficiency in my life and affairs.

8. My consciousness of the Spirit within me as my unlimited Source is the Divine Power to restore the years the locusts have eaten, to make all things new, to

lift me up to the High Road of abundant prosperity. This awareness, understanding and knowledge of Spirit, appears as every visible form and experience that I could possibly desire.

9. When I am aware of the God-Self within me as my total fulfilment, I am totally fulfilled. I am now aware of this Truth. I have found the secret of life, and I relax in the knowledge that the Activity of Divine Abundance is eternally operating in my life. I simply have to be aware of the flow, the radiation, of that Creative Energy, which is continuously, easily and effortlessly pouring forth from my Divine Consciousness. I am now aware. I am now in the flow.

10. I keep my mind and thoughts off "this world" and I place my entire focus on God within as the only Cause of my prosperity. I acknowledge the Inner Presence as the only activity in my financial affairs, as the substance of all things visible. I place my faith in the Principle of Abundance in action within me.

The Abundance Book by John Randolph Price

SUMMARY: IDENTITY – WHO ARE YOU?

- Identity is a label that you use to describe yourself and others. The question is these labels are they negative or positive?
- Remember no one can make you feel inferior without your consent.
- Opinions are not facts, hear them and let them go. It's like a loaf of bread, no matter how thin you slice it there will always be two sides to it.
- People can say what they like about you or call you all the names under the sun but it's up to you how you choose to response in a given moment.
- Incantations are similar to Affirmations but much more powerful in changing, re-wiring and re-conditioning your old identities with a brand new one.
- Remember Incantation/Affirmation without DISCIPLINE is the beginning of INSANITY.
- There are 6 key factors to make your new identity work.
- Emotions – Don't just recite it or write it down, play some of your favourite songs and connect emotions with the words you are saying to really bring it to life.
- Consistency – Don't just do it once or twice, make it a daily habit. To start you off, you need to do it for 90 days and continue after that, so it becomes a way of life, a way of living.
- Poetic – If you can make the words rhyme or create a lyric out of your new identity then great. One of my clients sings her incantations every day.
- Reward – Make sure you encourage yourself by rewarding yourself for the small wins along the way. After 30-day reward yourself and after 60 days do the same again and after 90 days definitely reward yourself

and continue to do so every month after that. It gives you something to look forward to whilst completely re-programming your brain and mind to creating the life you truly deserve.

- Sameness – Don't keep changing your new identity or incantation because it will confuse your unconscious mind. Be very clear what you want to give, be, do and have before you commit it to paper and stick with it until you have achieved.

- Accountability – If you are serious about creating a life by design then make yourself accountable and responsible for creating it by finding an accountability partner that would hold you to higher standards – Not someone who will let you off the hook each time you failed to deliver on your promise to yourself.

- Remember your new identity or incantation could also act or double up as a big goal that you are wanting to achieve as well as a way of developing your character and attitude to become who you want to be. Make it a big scary, exciting and audacious goal that you have no idea how to achieve it. Now that's real thinking!!!

ABOUT THE AUTHOR
WHO IS OLUWATOSIN OGUNNUSI

I was born and raised in Lagos, Nigeria. My childhood experiences were one of lack and limitations. As a young boy of 13 years old, I remembered very vividly when my dad told my stepbrother and I that he could no longer afford to send us to school. It was my worst nightmare, I asked, "What do you expect us to do instead? He replied, " I don't care what you do, you can become a bricklayer, carpenter or mechanic, take a pick.

To cut a long story short, that did not happen. My mother came to our rescue, thank God. She, got me and my stepbrother and I into a local state school, called, "Hope High School." After having attended a boarding school in the North of Nigeria called, "Federal Government College Mina. " For the first half, of my high school years, I always remembered the family, not having much money and hardly eating one square meal a day let alone two or three meals a day.

Throughout high school I was given the equivalent of £1.50 every day as my expenses, whilst all of my fellow students were given the equivalent of £5.00 per day. I had to spend 50p for getting a bus to school in the morning and spend 50p for lunch and 50p to get a bus back home after school. Most weeks, I would have to save my 50p for days and weeks to be able to join my schoolmates in buying a proper meal for lunch. The words, "I can't afford it, I don't have any money, you can't do that because it's too expensive," were the language my father used constantly in our household while I was growing up.

LONDON

I came to London in 1992 and put myself through college and through the persuasiveness of my father, I ended up studying and working as an Account's Assistant, which I didn't think suited my personality. I hated what I was doing, I knew I wanted to help and motivate people, but I didn't know how to do it as a career. Even though I had been involved in personal development throughout my accounting career.

So, the question is, "What kept me in a job that I didn't like for 8 years?"

My conditioning and my beliefs about who I was and what I was capable of had kept me limited in my thinking and playing small.

I believed the colour of my skin defined me and it made me feel inferior to others around me. I also believed money was the solution to all our problem - As we didn't have any and my father couldn't afford anything of importance for the family - Just the basic shelter, food and clothing and he couldn't even provide that on a consistent basis for the family. I even believed that I didn't have the right education because my father couldn't afford to send me to University and therefore, somehow, I had missed out on something that everybody else had and I didn't. So, I couldn't really relate to my colleagues at the time.

My whole conditioning was very negative to say the least, even after I had attended numerous seminar and events and knew that I was thinking in reverse regarding my circumstances and all I had to do was change the way I was thinking. Through attending these personal development seminars, I had acquired a lot of knowledge but it was all head knowledge. What do I mean?

You see intellectually, I knew what to and I was very good at impacting that knowledge on other people other than myself. Perhaps you can relate? You know what to do but you are not doing it. You were great at teaching others and they were getting great results, but you just couldn't translate that intellectual knowledge into an emotional connection within yourself.

So, I asked myself, where does one go from here? As you know knowing and not doing is equal to not knowing right?

As destiny would have it. Something miraculous happened. The Global drinks company (Seagram PLC) that I was working for at that time sold their drinks business and merged their entertainment side with a company called Vivendi Universal. Fortunately, for me I was made redundant as I worked in the drinks area. During the months leading to the redundancy I was given the opportunity to do a lot of personality profile testing on myself via the company – And it really opened my eyes and for the first time in my life at age 29 years of age. I started to really think about what it that I really wanted out of life. Before that I wasn't thinking for myself even though I thought I was – Everybody (My father, my mother, my friends, my bosses or anyone in authority) else were thinking for me. That was my old conditioning speaking to me inside my head, "Always listen to your elders because they know better than you." This is what we were told growing up as a child in my culture.

The irony was for the past 8 years I have been coaching and helping others get what they wanted and here I was filled up and crippled with "FEAR" of embarking on my own dreams, desires and goals. Have you ever felt like this? Anyway, it was at this stage of my life that I said to myself, "Enough now Tosin, It's time to stand up and be counted, it's time to face up to my limitations and change them forever. It's time to break free!

My whole life started to change and took a whole new direction from attending just one event (Life Success Training) with Bob Proctor. Meeting and training with Bob Proctor was a defining moment for me in my life. This was my first ever, "Personal Development Training" ever.

I remembered vividly an encounter with Bob at his preview event before the life-changing event, which I often share from the stage at my own events:

Picture this, you are in a huge seminar room that could hold 300 people and you are sat in the front row. And Bob walks up to me and says, "Who are you?"

And I proudly reply, "I'm Tosin Ogunnusi" as you do, and I was also pointing to my nametag that I had on at the time. Bob, looked directly at me and said, "That is not who you are, that's just a label that your parents gave you – When you were born you had no name."

He went on to someone else in the front row, and asked "Are you white?" The person in question duly answered, "Yes of course I am!" Bob replied, "No you're not white, my shirt is white as he had a white shirt on at the time."

Bob came back to me and said, "Are you black?" Now not wanting to state the obvious I said, "Yes I am black and proud." Bob replied, "You are not black, my shoes are black, he was wearing black leather shoes at the time."

Now, I don't know if you are like me, and the rest of the audience in attendance, we were all confused and perhaps you are too. If my name is not Tosin Ogunnusi and she's not white and I'm not black, then what the freaking hell are we right? This seems like the next logical question to ask right? That's when he dropped the bombshell and said something so profound that it literally obliterated all of my limiting beliefs in one sentence. It may just do the same for you. You might do well to commit this to memory by writing it down in your journal.

He said, "You and I and everyone else on this planet are SPIRITUAL beings having a HUMAN experience!" Wow! No one has ever put it that way for me, not ever. From that moment onwards, I stopped seeing and defining people by their colour, race, culture, religion or sex. I just saw people just like me period. We are all on this journey of exploration of ourselves. This was a huge breakthrough for me personally.

After 3 hours with Bob Proctor, I knew right there and then that I wanted to be trained by him. I went up to him and said, "Bob, thank you so much for such an enlightening and insightful event, I would very much like to do what you do." He looked directly at me as if he was searching into my soul. Then he said, "Son if you want to do what I do then go to the back of the room and sign up for your Life Success Training Program."

I said, "Okay, Bob but how much is it?" Bob replied, "It's £10,000."

I immediately shouted out loud, "What? £10,000 pounds, wow, I can't afford it. I haven't even saved up £500 at the time let alone £10,000."

Bob Proctor, allowed me to go through my dramatic moment and he didn't say a word during it. He just looked at me intently and paused. When it appeared that I was somehow calmer he looked straight into my eyes and said, "Son, if you can't afford it then you can't afford not to!" And he turned around and walked away from me I was left standing there thinking to myself, how rude just to walk away from someone like that.

When I look back now, I believe Bob did me a huge favour by saying what he did and walking away – Because what he was really saying was, "Son don't waste my time and don't give me all your excuses, if you really want to change your life and do something then get off your backside and do something about it period." Isn't that true for all of us? If you really want something and it means a lot to you and you are totally interested in it, you usually find a way, don't you? Well that's exactly what I did! I found a way. I took my redundancy pay of 2 and a half years and I went to Barclays Bank for a loan that took me 8 years to pay back.

My whole family thought I was crazy when I spent all my redundancy money and the Barclays loan on one training event with Bob Proctor. I have to admit and be totally honest even I thought to myself, "Tosin, you are crazy, and I think you need your head examined!"

I certainly don't have those thoughts anymore because that investment in myself at the age of 29 has literally changed my life, as it was my turning point and pivotal moment in my life. It ignited my passion for pursuing my dreams and made me hungry for learning and improving myself.

Later that year I attended Tony Robbins flagship event, "UPW -Unleash the Power Within," Totally loved it, especially Tony's energy. I believed my gift was my energy and I wanted to use it to inspire others. I loved UPW so much that I attended the event 9 times. I crewed the event 4 times and attended it 5 times. It really opened my eyes to how Tony works plus I attended his mastery university events as well. Tony's style had a huge impact on me as well as Bob's.

My number one goal at the time was to find a way to combine Tony's energy and training style with Bob Proctor's style. So, I set an outcome to find someone in the UK doing exactly what Tony was doing with UPW. This is how I met Andy Harrington a great business turnaround coach. It was during my time with him that I discovered NLP (Neuro Linguistic Programming). It was here that I got to study and learn about the work of Richard Bandler and John Grinder (the creators of NLP), which is simply the study of human excellence.

I became an NLP Trainer in 2006 and had extensive study and coaching from one the world's best NLP Master Trainers

(Topher Morrrison) from Tampa, Florida. Topher Morrison was the person responsible for giving me the opportunity to teach NLP to others and for that I would be truly indebted to him.

Since then I have personally started and co-founded 4 different companies that didn't quite make it as I would like but I learnt so much about myself in terms of my weaknesses and strengthens.

Today, we operate internationally under the Umbrella of Mpowerment (www.mpowerment.co.uk).

I have been extremely fortunate, to have grown tremendously from the shy, timid 19-year-old who arrived in the UK in 1992 to the person that I am today. When I arrived, I felt inferior to others, I didn't belief in myself and I couldn't lead a silent prayer in front of a small group of people because I use to stammer. So, say, I was a bad shape is putting it mildly. Most people who know me would like to believe that I should be further on than I am right now, but the truth of the matter is, if they only knew where I was back then and where I am right now – Wow! It's like night and day.

I personally consider myself to be a work-in-progress. I have a personal prayer that I say to my maker (God, Origin or Source) whatever name you choose to give it. And it goes like this, "Thank you God, that I am not where I use to be but dear Lord I am nowhere near where I need to be! Thank you for the continued learning, challenges and opportunities to grow. Amen!"

Over the years I have had a lot of personal achievements but some stood-out than most, here are the ones that I'm personally proud of, from little old me an ordinary guy who decided to make a difference in the world (this could be you too):

- Winning the NLPer of the year 2011 award from the APCTC (Association of Professional Coaches, Trainers and Consultants). Your own per group in the Personal Development Industry voting for you. It's very satisfying when others in the industry recognises your efforts and your clients get the results they've paid you for.
- Winning Trainer of the year 2016 from the PSA (Professional Speakers Academy).
- One of my proudest moments was when I was inspired to create the "Time 2 Break Free Life System" in 2016, which is responsible for writing this book.

Life has given a lot over the years and it's now time to start giving back to life and humanity as a whole. Here's a snap shoot of what I am really about:

PURPOSE

My purpose in life is to use my gift (which is my energy, creativity and enthusiasm) to make a positive impact/difference in the world, by inspiring and transforming other people's lives and being an instrument/catalyst for change. This is the reason why I was born.

PASSION

My passion is adding value by helping others to improve their performance in all areas of life.

CORE BELIEFS

My core belief is that we are all empowered beings/souls that have been endowed with the seeds of greatness to succeed from birth, both in this lifetime and beyond.

MISSION & VISION

My Mission and Vision is to inspire and empower people and businesses to reach greater/higher levels of performance and achievements – And to be a leading global brand in the Personal Development Industry.

COMPANY VALUES

My Company Values are a) Adventure b) Contribution and c) Energy

ADVENTURE

As a company adventure for us signifies having fun, challenge and excitement into our training programs as a lover of variety, I believe that variety is the spice of life. Training and working with people from all walks of life is an adventure for us. We love people, cultures and places. Hence why we love working in different countries and continents around the world.

CONTRIBUTION

Contribution for us is about family and giving back real value to our customers, clients and mentees. Contribution is also about reaching out to others less fortunate than us. It's our way of saying thank you by sharing our resources (money, talents, gifts and skills) to help give another human being an opportunity that they would not have had, had we not intervened. This is very important to us as a company. It also means leading by example and showing others that anything is possible once you put your mind to it, stay focused and consistent and keep pushing the boundaries. Then you can give more, be more, do more and have more in your life.

ENERGY

This is our essence, our true gift as a company. We put 100 per cent energy into everything we do. Energy is about giving our clients, customers and mentees the very best of ourselves and in turn we can demand them to give us their very best in return. It's all about attention focused driven values.

OTHER PROGRAMS BY THE AUTHOR

2 Days Time 2 Break Free Bootcamp

A unique opportunity for you and your team to experience the awesome power of this book by going through our "Time 2 Break Free Life System." This will be one of the best weekends you've ever spent. Taking on the "B (Board Breaking) R (Re-Bar Bending) A (Arrow Breaking) G(Glass walking) & F (Firewalking)" challenge.

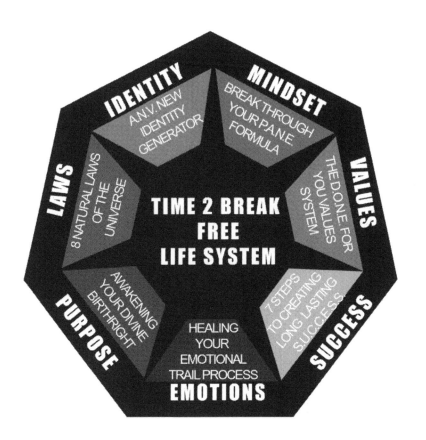

12 Months Speaking & Presenting with IMPACT Mentoring Program

Learn how to:

1. Speak and present with impact

2. Structure your talk and presentations

3. Engage your audience

Using our F1 Speaker System:

F1 SPEAKER SYSTEM

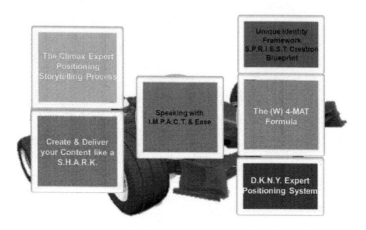

4 Days Empowerment Activities Instructor Training

Learn how to take individuals and groups through the Empowerment Activities (Board Breaking, Re-Bar Bending, Arrow Breaking, Glass Walking and Firewalking) – And as result see how you can impact lives at a profound level.

Let us take you through our "CLASP Your Team System."

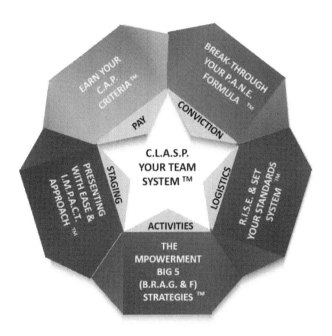

For further information about the above training programs check out our website: www.mpowerment.co.uk and follow us on social media:

www.facebook.com/mpowermenttosin

www.twitter.com/MpowermentTosin

www.instagram.com/mpowermenttosin

Time 2 Break Free Mobile App coming soon.

PRAISES FOR "TIME 2 BREAK FREE!"

"Time 2 Break Free is a must read book if you want to understand yourself better, improve your life, turn adversity into success and achieve a lot more. You will be glad you read it".

Mac Attram - #1 International Best Selling Author (Face It & Fix It)

Tosin as the master communicator that he is, has taken a wealth of wisdom and crafted it into a book that caters for all our learning preferences, packed with information, exercises and concise summaries.

This is a must read for anyone that wants to truly understand what holds them back from having, doing and being anything they want in Life AND even more importantly - How to Break Free!

Harry Singha - The Speaker Coach & Philanthropist (2017 Global Humanitarian Award Winner) www.HarrySingha.com

Time To Break Fee is a book about breaking free from setbacks. If you are thinking of how to take your life and career to the next level or break free from living a life of mediocrity and unfulfilled dreams, this is a book for you. The book will teach you how to break free from doubt and achieve your full potential. In this book, Tosin shares 7 powerful principles that if applied would transformed your live to greater heights. It is a practical book, written in a simple easy to read style for all ages to enjoy. It is a must-read for anyone motivated to improving, their lives. It shows how anyone can aim high, move fast and excel.

Don't just read the book, but implementation of the ideas in this book is where the true power of this book resides. So, take immediate action on the ideas in this book and it will change the course and direction of your life. I highly recommend this book.

Dr Dayo Olomu, Motivational Speaker, Author, Trainer, Leadership Coach is the Vice Chair, CIPD South London; Founder, Dayo Olomu Foundation and board member, Southwark Diocesan Board of Education.

What a book! It is full of hidden secrets that can bless millions of people that are living in bondage. There is no better person to write the book than my friend Tosin Ogunnusi.

I shared a part of my life with him when he joined my secondary school then (Hope high school). I believed that was a traumatic period of his life. Tosin's family was struggling financially.

Looking back now, it was obvious my friend has talent. I am excited that talent has been unfolded now and he has peace doing what he loves doing. The book will be a blessing to millions who are going through self-limitations. It will liberate those who have not discovered their true identity. It will be a guiding light to those who want to fulfil their destiny.

I have no reservations in recommending this book to everyone.

Oluwagbenga Adeoye - Financial Controller, Union Bank of Nigeria

In this practical book, Tosin takes you through his journey, indulging all of your senses as he shares his wisdom from his own perspective and experience.

His passion for NLP and other learning's will put you through processes, doing mini exercises that create breakthroughs as you go along keep you engaged.

I first met Tosin around 1999 at an Amyn Dahya event and our friendship has flourished ever since. He always talked about making a difference and it makes me proud when I think of the incredible difference he is making to so many people today.

Tosin has put himself through the painful process of breaking himself up and reinventing himself on numerous occasions so that he can serve better. His positive attitude and commitment to constant growth has led him to great height and yet, something deep inside tells me he has not even started.

He asked me to be the best man at his wedding and I felt so honored, I remember thinking about our beautiful friendship and moments shared, I spent a few moments reflecting on our journey to that point and a few tears rolled down my face. Tosin is a kind-hearted soul, a gentleman and his passion for life is second to none. He is a Yes to life and his book reflects this, by the time you are finished with it, you too will have shifted your life to the next level for you.

To Making A Difference, Love & Success Always - Kalpesh Patel X

Tosin Ogunnusi hailing from Nigeria is the King of Empowerment and Motivation. For as long as I can remember he has been working his motivational brand of magic to enhance lives. In *'Time to Break Free,'* Tosin captures the fiery passion inherent in his name, and seen in the flame color attire he is known for. This book challenges you to break free, find your purpose and ignite your own fire. He shares a multitude of ways you can make massive, positive shifts in your life, break free of your constraints and live the life of your dreams. A must, get your copy now!

Caroline Shola Arewa – International Coach, Speaker, Trainer and Author of Energy 4 Life

Wow, this book really is an awesome resource. It's like having a blueprint for success right in your hands.

Not only is it easy to understand because the process is so intuitive but the questions and exercises are so practical and relative. They really require you to go within and think deeply and congruently to reveal your true self.

As a self proclaimed Personal Development Coach myself I can tell you that this book will be a number one go to for me for years to come.

Ben Jobson - Inspirational Speaker and Founder www.way2go.net.au

Tosin is a genuinely motivating individual and the methodology in this book will enable you to break free from the norm and create the life you deserve.

Andy Harrington – World-Class Public Speaking Expert and Sunday Times Bestselling Author (Passion Into Profit)

"Time to break free" will literary change your life forever! Tosin Ogunnusi writes like he speaks and shoots from the hip. This book of personal development will challenge your mind, your heart, all your senses, and emotions and make you rethink some aspects of your life. It will also make you hungry for more... Read it if you want to "Raise Your Game to limitless levels!"

Gilles Amadou Acogny - Co-Founder and CEO Acosphere Ltd. (A global) Management consultancy firm based in London.

Tosin's book Time to Break Free is a very powerful tool on one's way of self-development. It inspired me, taught me and made me ask myself important questions. What I especially liked is the way Tosin works with stories here. His stories and examples he serves us bring joy and valuable insights at the same time. The language is nice and easy to read. Finally and most importantly: this book heals. I catch myself looking forward to find some time to read more. It helped me in a tough moment and in fact empowered me. Now I know that I really CAN create a life I wish and deserve. Time to break free by Tosin Ogunnusi is definitely the book you must read.

Libuse Kalova – Easy Software – Prague

What a brilliant book (Time To Break Free). It seeks to help you as a reader breakthrough and break out of the limitations we all subconsciously have. It's amazing how we choose the books we read based on what problems we have. However, the author has described how every human being can break through their own personal glass ceiling regardless of how successful they are, even when there's no obvious problem. His style of writing makes the book easy to digest. I love the summaries at the end of each chapter as one can go back and review the whole book several times. This makes it a useful resource for anyone looking to achieve more and assess their blocks and progresses periodically.

Ola Adesanoye, Parent and Child Education Coach

"The best thing ever is when you encounter teachers who are willing to give genuinely and openly and that's what Tosin is doing in his book.

He's sharing his knowledge and experience of years in the personal development sector and he's not holding back.

In a time when humankind is in so much need for such information to heal and grow, I can only recommend his book to sit by your bed side table and applaud his generosity, care and kindness that you just can't miss reading his book "

Nezha Boussetta – Empowerment Coach, Bordeaux, France.

In life we all hold conditions & stories inside weighing us down whether it be from adversity tragedy or childhood - in this book Time to Break free Tosin has poured all his knowledge & wisdom into giving you all the tools to finally release the weight you have been carrying that weighs you down. A book you will return to again and again as you heal on different levels and are able to create a new life of new possibilities - highly recommended

Roslyn bell - Entrepreneur speaker & author

"Tosin is amazing in showing you how to unleash your power, uncover your dreams and reach your goals. He knows this path by heart, and in his book he shares the steps to unleash your power. No matter where you are right now, prepare yourself for a big leap."

Denisa Riha Paleckova - Sex and Relationship Expert

The road to self-improvement is long and not always straightforward.

Tosin Ogunnusi's 'Time 2 Break Free' book encourages readers to overcome fear and be persistent in a journey among the unknown. It is a fantastic read for anyone who wants to have mastery over his or her own life.

In a world where we are facing challenges everyday, this book is really helpful to get you to focus on what's important and will help you not only overcome your challenges, but also will help you find your purpose and accomplish your goals.

Shelina Mawji -Well-being Coach- Press Pause.

Tosin has somehow managed to cram literally hundreds of thousands of pounds worth of coaching and training into one book! If you're just starting on your personal development journey, or you've already started and are looking for advanced insights, this is a must read!

Nick James - International Speaker - CEO and Founder of Expert Empires.

"Tosin is the master of motivation, his infectious energy and the rhythmic pitch of his voice makes all in the room stand up, listen and manifest change. This book is superb riddled with golden nuggets and a-ha moments that will certainly help you break free!"

Ketan Makwana (Serial Entrepreneur, International Speaker & Mentor)

Tosin's incredible understanding of the world, people and human nature makes him the ultimate Empowerment coach. He knows what it takes to make people excel and achieve great success. This book was a fantastic read. Tosin really has excelled in providing such valuable information for the readers. Are you lacking purpose in your life? Do you want to learn how you can train your mind to consistently achieve results? Well look no further, this book is a must read for you!

Mayooran Senthilmani - Finance Director, Author & Publisher

I have experienced Tosin's Seminars and firewalks with over 1,000 of my team and people in the care sector over many years - His new book (Time 2 Break Free) shows his personal journey of transforming his life and giving the reader practical tips and ideas on transforming their own life's to the next level!

Avnish Goyal - Chair of Hallmark Care Homes

"TIME 2 BREAK is an absolute breath of FRESH AIR upon so many levels. Tosin's depth of wisdom, mastery and knowledge are the exact truth that can be the difference that makes the difference in your life not to mention his high energy, fun personality and commitment towards transforming lives. Myself and family are long term client of Tosin and I highly recommend Tosin Ogunnusi's products and services."

Sabrina Ben Salmi BSc - Award Winning Author, Multi-Award Winner, Mamas Secret Recipe, 21 Day Shift Happens

Tosin has focused on what he refers to as the 7 leadership principles, Mindset, Values, Success, Emotions, Purpose, Universal Laws and Seld Identity. In doing so Tosin explains concepts, and ideas of how you can heal and express your emotions, discover your purpose, set goals and achieve them, manage your emotions, live your life on your own terms and icorporate his 8 universal laws.

Sanjeev Desour property & Private Equity Investor

Easy Project - The best project management tools in one application

Easy Project is based on **WBS, Gantt, Agile methods, Earned Value and other best project management practices.** It is compatible with modules for Resources, Finances, Help Desk and CRM.

Run your projects, manage your finances, resources and clients data all in one application – simply and more effectively. Increase efficiency and profit by saving time and using your resources smartly.

To learn more, please visit our website:

www.mpowerment.co.uk/project-management

Cannadorra – Hemp for my Health

Cannadora offers high quality hemp products – CBD hemp oils, hemp tea, hemp oils, hemp seeds, proteins, salts, ointments, cometics and others.

With over 20 000 customers worldwide and EU certified and BIO products, Cannadorra has become one of the leaders on the hemp market.

To learn more, please visit our website:
www.mpowerment.co.uk/hemp

Printed in Great Britain
by Amazon